Pastoral Reflections on Life and Ministry

Pastoral Reflections on Life and Ministry

JOHN P. DAVIS

Foreword by Andrew Straubel

RESOURCE *Publications* · Eugene, Oregon

PASTORAL REFLECTIONS ON LIFE AND MINISTRY

Copyright © 2021 John P. Davis. All rights reserved. Except for brief quotations in critical publications or reviews, no part of this book may be reproduced in any manner without prior written permission from the publisher. Write: Permissions, Wipf and Stock Publishers, 199 W. 8th Ave., Suite 3, Eugene, OR 97401.

Resource Publications
An Imprint of Wipf and Stock Publishers
199 W. 8th Ave., Suite 3
Eugene, OR 97401

www.wipfandstock.com

PAPERBACK ISBN: 978-1-6667-3101-9
HARDCOVER ISBN: 978-1-6667-2307-6
EBOOK ISBN: 978-1-6667-2308-3

10/27/21

Contents

Foreword by Andrew Straubel — ix
Preface — xi

SECTION ONE | ON THE GOSPEL

Chapter One: What is the Gospel? — 3
Chapter Two: What is Gospel-Centered? — 9
Chapter Three: Jesus is the Same — 12
Chapter Four: The Real Jesus — 15
Chapter Five: Are All "Faiths" Equal? — 18
Chapter Six: The Transcendent Joy of the Gospel — 20
Chapter Seven: Four Cries of the Soul — 22

SECTION TWO | ON THEOLOGY

Chapter Eight: Jesus—God's Final and Full Revelation — 27
Chapter Nine: The Sufficiency of the Word of God — 31
Chapter Ten: The "Already, Not Yet," Kingdom of Jesus Christ — 33
Chapter Eleven: Acquiring Knowledge of God — 35
Chapter Twelve: Resurrection Hope — 38
Chapter Thirteen: The Human Condition — 41
Chapter Fourteen: Unity, Despite Theological Difference — 43
Chapter Fifteen: The Continuity of Theological Concepts — 48
Chapter Sixteen: God: The Perfect Theologian — 52
Chapter Seventeen: Divine Sovereignty and Human Freedom — 55
Chapter Eighteen: Calvinism on the "N" Train — 64
Chapter Nineteen: My *ordo salutis* on the "N" Train — 69

Contents

SECTION THREE | ON SANCTIFICATION

Chapter Twenty: The Gospel and Transformation — 77
Chapter Twenty-One: How Does the Gospel Transform Us? — 83
Chapter Twenty-Two: The Congruence of Grace and Discipleship — 87
Chapter Twenty-Three: Growing Up into Salvation — 89
Chapter Twenty-Four: "My cross to bear" — 91
Chapter Twenty-Five: Clarifying the "Means of Grace" — 93

SECTION FOUR | ON CHRISTIAN FELLOWSHIP

Chapter Twenty-Six: Christian Fellowship on the "N" Train — 99
Chapter Twenty-Seven: Gospel-Centered Tier One Fellowship — 104
Chapter Twenty-Eight: A Gospel-Centered Way Beyond Fundamentalism and New Evangelicalism — 106

SECTION FIVE | ON PASTORAL MINISTRY

Chapter Twenty-Nine: On Personality, Power, Friendship, and Integrity — 113
Chapter Thirty: Ordinary Pastors — 116
Chapter Thirty-One: Extended Sabbaticals — 118
Chapter Thirty-Two: Reflections on Preaching — 120
Chapter Thirty-Three: Factors that Shape Life and Ministry in the Local Church — 122
Chapter Thirty-Four: Why I Continue to Evangelize Other Christians — 125
Chapter Thirty-Five: Obsession with Urban Church Planting — 128
Chapter Thirty-Six: The True Value of My Life's Work — 131
Chapter Thirty-Seven: What I would look for in a Seminary! — 133

SECTION SIX | ON ECCLESIOLOGY

Chapter Thirty-Eight: New Covenant Israel in the City — 137
Chapter Thirty-Nine: Why we use the Apostles' Creed at Grace Church of Philly — 139
Chapter Forty: A Community of Witness — 141

Contents

SECTION SEVEN | ON ECCLESIOLOGY

Chapter Forty-One: "catholicity"—Institutional, Incarnational, or Impossible	145
Chapter Forty-Two: The Weekly Celebration of the Lord's Table	148
Chapter Forty-Three: A Qualified Egalitarianism	150
Chapter Forty-Four: Baptism and Church Membership	153
Chapter Forty-Five: Gospel-Centered Church Leadership	157

SECTION EIGHT | ON SOCIAL ISSUES

Chapter Forty-Six: Conservative or Liberal under the Lordship of Jesus Christ	161
Chapter Forty-Seven: The Politics of Jesus and Peter	164
Chapter Forty-Eight: Seven reasons why I do not join the popular, secular fight against racism!	167
Chapter Forty-Nine: Sandy Hook and the Gospel	169
Chapter Fifty: "as a matter of fairness"	171
Bibliography	173

Foreword

Dr. John P. Davis has been a pastor and friend for over forty years. He has pastored churches from suburbia to the inner city. He has crossed ethnic and cultural lines that few have ever attempted to cross. And now he has come back to share what he has learned. To those who know him he is a leader among leaders. His book, *Pastoral Reflections on Life and Ministry*, provides a wealth of theological insight, clarifies a host of contemporary issues, and offers practical advice that few possess.

The opening chapter on the gospel sets the tone for the entire work. For as long as I have known Dr. Davis, the gospel has been at the center of his entire ministry. In fact, he is the most gospel centered pastor that I have ever known. He talks about the gospel all the time! He writes about the gospel all the time. And he preaches the gospel all the time. And he lives out the gospel also.

Men in ministry or those considering pastoral ministry will greatly benefit from this work. Dr. Davis is standing at the end of a long journey and now turns around to share what he has learned. In my experience this is rare. I so appreciated the clarity and conviction brought out in Section Two: Theology-Scriptural authority and sufficiency, God's Sovereignty vs. Free Will, the "Already-Not-Yet" aspects of the Kingdom of God. His eye opening experience on the "N Train" is heart-warming as he allows God to break his heart for the world. And, I especially enjoyed the chapter on Ordinary Pastors. I am one of them.

Years ago while struggling in a small church I began to question my pastoral call. I called Pastor Davis and we talked. He reminded

Foreword

me of a number of things and that my life was an investment for God. All the education and all the experience I had gained was for a reason. It had a purpose whether I realized it or not. I needed those words that day and it kept me going. We are told to "run the race that is set before us!" And, we are to run our race! We are not to look around at others. Dr. John Davis' work, *Pastoral Reflections on Life and Ministry*, grants us a look into one man's race; and no doubt there is a crown awaiting him on the day he meets his Savior face to face.

Andrew Straubel, an Ordinary Pastor

Preface

I have been a pastor for over 45 years, planting my first church when I was just out of college in 1975. I was 24 years old, equipped with a bachelor's degree in Bible and a fair competency in Greek. I was ready to take on the world of church planting. Or, so I thought. It did not take long for me to realize that I needed both maturity in life and a deeper and broader theological education. Over the next twenty-seven years I continued my education acquiring an MDiv and ThM and a DMin,

I continued pastoring and church planting while advancing my theological education. Over these 45 years of ministry, I have pastored in affluent, suburban, mono-cultural churches, older more traditional churches, and multi-ethnic urban churches. I've said over the years that I would not write and publish until I was over sixty, because by then my theology and understanding of the Bible would be settled.

Well, here I am at 70 years old writing this preface to *Pastoral Reflections on Life and Ministry*. I am sure that what I write today sounds much different than what I might have said 45 years ago. My theology and understanding of the Bible is not completely settled but it is much more mature and balanced after all these years.

I am still learning, reading and studying daily. My mind is still inquisitive. I still have unanswered questions. If God allows me many more years of serving Him, I may say some things differently in the future. I hold the conviction that anything I presently believe is negotiable when the Word of God convinces me otherwise.

Preface

I hope and pray that these various reflections on life, theology, and ministry may provoke you to think about these things, formulate your own thoughts, write them down, and share them with others.

Blessings in Jesus' Name,
John P. Davis

SECTION ONE

On the Gospel

CHAPTER ONE

What is the Gospel?

The gospel is the proclamation of good news that the promised Messiah/Deliverer has come and that His name is Jesus. This proclamation of good news is rooted in the Old Testament promise of the Messiah/Deliverer who comes in both suffering and glory to rescue mankind and the cosmos from the effects of Adam's rebellion and the resultant curse.

The gospel is the good news about what a holy and sovereign God has accomplished for sinners in the person and work of Jesus Christ.

Without diminishing other aspects of the good news that the promised Messiah/Deliverer has come, we understand that the heart of the gospel is that Jesus lived the life that we failed to live, died the death that we deserve to die, and rose again to restore the life we forfeited because of our sin.

According to Galatians 1:4 the gospel is about the one "... who gave himself for our sins to deliver us from the present evil age, according to the will of our God and Father . . . ." God's Gospel is about substitutionary sacrifice. about deliverance from sin. And about eschatology, i.e., delivered from this age to the new age.

"The gospel" is equivalent to "the grace of Christ."

> ⁶I am astonished that you are so quickly deserting him who called you in the grace of Christ and are turning to a different gospel . . . (Gal 1).

Grace is the unfettered goodness of God, i.e., His generosity to the undeserving. His grace is so amazing it will take the ages to come to unpack the richness of that grace (Eph 2:7). We appreciate grace more and more as we see our deep sinfulness and His great holiness, as we see our desperate need and His generous provision.

At the heart of grace is Christ, i.e., "the grace of Christ." Christ is the essence of grace, the one who displays grace, and who gives grace.

It is by the grace of Christ through which we are called into a relationship with God.

IMPLICATIONS OF THE GOSPEL IN GALATIANS.

Let me briefly suggest some of those implications from reading through the Epistle to the Galatians.

1. Getting the gospel wrong affects how you see Christian community.

When something other than the gospel is elevated among Christians, unity in Christ is threatened. In Galatians 2:14–16 we see how Peter failed to live out the implications of the gospel of grace. Even though he knew that the gospel of Christ removed the barrier between Jew and Gentile and that the ceremonial practices of the Old Covenant were abolished in Christ, he broke fellowship with Gentile believers because of the influence of those who set forth law-keeping as a measure of one's standing with God.

In the gospel we dance in celebration together over the victory accomplished in the death and resurrection of Jesus Christ, not over our preference for theological systems or denominational labels or ethnocentricities or idiosyncratic church expectations.

2. Getting the gospel wrong affects how you see your standing with God.

When something other than the gospel is elevated in my life, I attempt to achieve my own righteous standing before God rather than resting in the finished work of Christ. Paul's extensive discussion in chapter 3 clearly sets forth the antithesis of human effort to the finished work of Christ. Either one's standing with God is an unfinished process being achieved through human effort or one stands fully accepted through faith in the finished work of Christ. The gospel declares that we are fully accepted through Jesus Christ. Consequently, we do not live with the burden of trying to achieve our own righteousness nor do we live in fear of God's rejection.

3. Getting the gospel wrong affects how you read and understand the Bible.

When something else other than the gospel is elevated in your hermeneutic, you may misread the OT. When the centrality of the gospel of Christ is marginalized or minimized, we read the Old Testament as a handbook on morals, a compilation of character studies, a history of a chosen ethnic people, and not the story of God's preparation of the world for Jesus Christ.

In some sense, the coming of Christ and His work of redemption creates a new hermeneutic. Were you to read the OT apart from the NT, you would come to radically different conclusions on concepts of temple, land, chosen people, obedience, eschatology—all of which are redefined by the gospel of Jesus Christ.

Chapter Three suggests that without the gospel we misunderstand the promise to Abraham in not recognizing that the quintessential seed of Abraham is Jesus Christ. He alone is the inheritor of the promise and all of those who have faith in Him share that inheritance.

Chapter Four suggests that without the gospel we misunderstand the institutions of ancient Israel and the nature of the law. In Paul's discussion of Hagar and Sara he takes an unexpected turn in interpreting the history of the Old Covenant people. We would expect the law (Mt. Sinai) and earthly Jerusalem to be associated with Sara the wife of Abraham and mother of Isaac, the progeny through which the promise comes. Rather these sacred institutions of Ancient Israel are identified with Hagar and with words like "of the flesh, slavery, earthly," while Sara is associated with promise and because of promise "our mother is the Jerusalem that is above."

No one reading the Old Testament without the vantage point of the gospel of Christ's finished work would come to the conclusions that Paul does in Galatians 4. As has been said for ages, "The New Testament is in the Old Testament concealed; the Old Testament is in the New Testament revealed." The gospel informs our reading of the Old Testament and enables us to see its proper place in the progress of redemption. Graeme Goldsworthy nicely sums up the relationship of Jesus Christ to the OT:

> The New Testament emphasizes the historic person of Christ and what he did for us, through faith, to become the friends of God. The emphasis is also on him as the one who sums up and brings to their fitting climax all the promises and expectations raised in the Old Testament. There is a priority of order here, which we must take into account if we are to understand the Bible correctly. It is the gospel event, as that which brings about faith in the people of God, that will motivate, direct, pattern, and empower the life of the Christian community. So we start from the gospel and move to an understanding of Christian living, and the final goal toward which we are moving.
>
> Again, we start from the gospel and move back into the Old Testament to see what lies behind the person and work of Christ. The Old Testament is not completely superseded by the gospel, for that would make it irrelevant to us. It helps us understand the gospel by showing us the origins and meanings of the various ideas and special words used to describe Christ and his works in the New Testament. Yet we must also recognize that Christ is God's fullest and final Word to mankind. As such he reveals to us the final meaning of the Old Testament.[1]

---

1. Goldsworthy, *According to Plan*, 106–7.

4. Getting the gospel wrong affects how you live the Christian life.

When something else other than the gospel is elevated in your living, self-effort rather than the power of the gospel becomes the focus of the Christian life. Chapter five of Galatians reminds us that the Christian life easily becomes a matter of legalism, or spiritual disciplines, or struggling against the flesh, rather than freedom through the victory accomplished by Christ on the cross. If the gospel is central in living out the Christian life it leads to a life lived in humility; if human effort is central in living out the Christian life, it inevitably leads to pride. J.I. Packer notes:

> ... the focus of health in the soul is humility, while the root of inward corruption is pride. In the spiritual life, nothing stands still. If we are not constantly growing downward into humility, we shall be steadily swelling up and running to seed under the influence of pride.[2]

Only the gospel of grace leads to humility because it reminds us daily of our inability to earn God's favor and of our need of His grace and mercy. Contemplation on the finished work of Christ is the means the Spirit employs to transform the life of a believer.

> [1]*For freedom Christ has set us free; stand firm therefore, and do not submit again to a yoke of slavery (Gal 5).*

5. Getting the gospel wrong affects the purpose of your life.

When something else other than the gospel is elevated in your focus, you bring glory to yourself and not the God of glory. In chapter two I will talk about the inadequacy of both the soteriological and doxological purposes of life. If my primary focus is on evangelism (soteriological) or of glorifying God by obedience (doxological), then my focus is on human effort, leading to either pride of success or shame of failure. If my focus is on the gospel, then I live

---

2. Packer, *Rediscovering Holiness*, 37.

in humility and joyful acceptance with the outcome of being concerned for evangelism and living a life in which God is glorified.

> [14]But far be it from me to boast except in the cross of our Lord Jesus Christ, by which the world has been crucified to me, and I to the world (Gal 6).

We should always be about the gospel so that glory will never be in our programs, or agendas, or successes, but in God who calls us in the grace of Jesus Christ. It is the gospel that is the underpinning for all we do, the driving force behind everything, the fulcrum by which we hold in balance everything else.

Furthermore, the gospel has implications at numerous levels:

- Personal—the gospel is about the most passionate love, the deepest mercy, the most magnificent grace, the most underserving forgiveness, and the greatest transforming power—all because of the death and resurrection of Jesus Christ.

- Church—the gospel creates a new community of believers whose lives corporately reflect the most passionate love, the deepest mercy, the most magnificent grace, the most underserving forgiveness, and the greatest transforming power.

- Societal—the gospel takes transformed individuals living in transformed community to effect incremental transformation in all areas of society that have been affected by the ravages of human rebellion and idolatry.

- Cosmic—the gospel guarantees the consummate transformation of all things at the Second Coming of Christ in the ushering in of the New Heavens and the New Earth.

CHAPTER TWO

What is Gospel-Centered?

Paul, said, "the gospel is of first importance" in the church (1 Cor 15:3–4). The gospel defines how we live out our ultimate purpose in life which is to glorify God in all things. In my early experience as a student and pastor, I was taught two alternative purposes for the world and for what drives the Christian life. I was taught that history has either a soteriological purpose (to redeem sinners) or a doxological purpose (to bring glory to God). Consequently, on the practical level, believers have either a soteriological purpose or a doxological purpose, i.e. either we are driven by our evangelistic passion to bring people to Christ or driven by our desire to bring glory to God by our obedience.

I am not focusing on the contrasting purposes in human history but on the practical outworking of those purposes. However, I would note that God's doxological purpose in human history is not achieved without his redemptive purposes being accomplished and, at the center of his doxological purpose is the redemption accomplished through the death and resurrection of Jesus Christ.

I am most interested in the practical outworking of how we understand our purpose in life. Formerly for me on the practical level, the soteriological purpose was eschewed because it focused on only one area of obedience while the doxological purpose was extolled because it included all areas of obedience.

Now I conclude that both the soteriological and doxological purposes were somewhat skewed in how they were presented to me. I have observed that both of these purposes, easily end up being moralistic and focused on self-effort. The focus becomes either how much evangelism and I am doing or how obedient am I becoming. Churches are full of believers burdened with guilt and shame over not winning enough souls to Christ or not being obedient enough in every area of their lives. Please don't misunderstand me. I am not encouraging less evangelism or a relaxed attitude toward obedience. However, the way that many Christians understand and practice "living for souls" or "living for God's glory" may ultimately steal glory from God.

We will engage joyfully in evangelism and obedience as we rest in the finished work of Christ.

I am supremely interested in glorifying my Creator and Redeemer. We are created for God's glory (Rev 4:11) and we are to do all things in life for His glory (1 Cor 10:31). However, without being gospel-centered we seek our own glory. Being gospel-centered helps avoid legalism/moralism on the one hand, and on the other hand relativism/hedonism (Ca. Tim Keller).

Being gospel-centered keeps the focus from being on our own self-effort. Being gospel-centered reminds us of God's great holiness, our great sinfulness, and His great grace showed to us in the death and resurrection of Christ. The gospel is about what God has accomplished for sinners in Christ and He is most glorified when we believe in and rest in this gospel.

Being gospel-centered ensures that God receives the glory.

> [30] And because of him you are in Christ Jesus, who became to us wisdom from God, righteousness and sanctification and redemption, [31] so that, as it is written, "Let the one who boasts, boast in the Lord (1 Cor 1)

> [14] But far be it from me to boast except in the cross of our Lord Jesus Christ, by which the world has been crucified to me, and I to the world (Gal 6).

Let me make a little twist on one of John Piper's famous quotes: He says, "God is most glorified when I am most satisfied in Him."[1]

---

1. Piper, *Desiring God*, 9.

What is Gospel-Centered?

I agree with that though I will tweak it a little in saying that "God is most glorified when I am most centered (at rest) in the gospel." Being at rest in the gospel is being satisfied in Him.[2]

---

2. For a good reader on being gospel-centered, see http://timmybrister.com/2009/08/27/a-gospel-centered-reader/.

CHAPTER THREE

Jesus is the Same

JESUS CHRIST—THE SAME, YESTERDAY, TODAY, AND FOREVER (HEBREWS 13:8)

The immutability of Christ comforts and assures us through the inevitable changes of life. Life is full of changes—some for the better—some for the worse. In a world of rapid and unpredictable change, we know one who is the same, yesterday, today, and forever. This immutable character of Jesus Christ concludes the book of Hebrews in a similar way to how the book began. Listen to some of those beginning words:

> [8] ¶ But of the Son he says, "Your throne, O God, is forever and ever, the scepter of uprightness is the scepter of your kingdom. [9] You have loved righteousness and hated wickedness; therefore God, your God, has anointed you with the oil of gladness beyond your companions." [10] And, "You, Lord, laid the foundation of the earth in the beginning, and the heavens are the work of your hands; [11] they will perish, but you remain; they will all wear out like a garment, [12] like a robe you will roll them up, like a garment they will be changed. But you are the same, and your years will have no end" (Heb 1).

Is not this our comfort? He is the same. In a world where governments change, economies change, physical appearances change, friends changes, climates change (so I'm told). In a world of certain, but unpredictable change, what can you depend on?

This is the central question of the book of Hebrews and the central issue of life? WHO IS THIS IMMUTABLE JESUS? Is Jesus the same, yesterday, today, and forever? The resounding answer is "Jesus is the Same." As you read through the book of Hebrews you will find the following affirmations about the immutability of Jesus.

- He is the same son of God, image of the father, creator of heavens and earth.
- He is the same one who takes on humanity that he may experience death for every man,
- He is the same one who pioneers and blazes the trail of salvation for all who will follow Him.
- He is the same one who sanctifies us and is not ashamed to call us brothers and sisters.
- He is the same sympathetic Savior who triumphed over the Devil and who helps us in our temptation.
- He is the same apostle and high priest of our confession who builds the house of salvation in which we live.
- He is the same one who brings us to the throne of his father to find mercy and grace.
- He is the same one who gives the Promised rest for weary sinners.
- He is the same one who is of a priestly order that has no end.
- He is the same priest, holy, harmless, undefiled, made higher than the heavens.
- He is the same one who offers himself as a once for all sacrifice for sins.
- He is the same one in whose blood is your forgiveness of sins.
- He is the same one who brings you not to Mount Sinai and its holy wrath but to Mount Sion and that grand celestial celebration.

- He is the same one who disciplines you because he loves you.
- He is the same one whom saints of old have found to be faithful in life and death.
- He is the same one who is coming and who will fulfill everyone promise to his children.
- He is the same one who endured the hardship of the race but entered into the joy of victory.

He was all of this yesterday. He is all of this today. He will be all of this tomorrow. He will not change, never, ever, will He change. He is the same.

CHAPTER FOUR

The Real Jesus

Biblical scholars involved in the Jesus Seminar have difficulty finding "the Jesus of history." In their reading of the gospels, they have concluded that "maybe" there are about fifteen authentic sayings of Jesus that they can attribute to him. Though the Jesus Seminar works under the guise of ecumenical Christian scholarship, perhaps the real motivation to find "the Jesus of history" lies in the unregenerate mind's repulsion at the Jesus of the Bible.

Liberal scholars do not like the Jesus of the Bible. The Bible presents Jesus as the eternal Son of the Triune God, the Creator of the world, the exclusive Redeemer of fallen mankind, and the final Judge of the entire world. Listen to what some of the biblical authors wrote about Jesus:

> [1]In the beginning was the Word, and the Word was with God, and the Word was God. [2] He was in the beginning with God. [3] All things were made through Him, and without Him nothing was made that was made. [4] In Him was life, and the life was the light of men.... [14] The Word became flesh and made his dwelling among us. We have seen his glory, the glory of the One and Only, who came from the Father, full of grace and truth (John 1).

> [30]But of Him you are in Christ Jesus, who became for us wisdom from God—and righteousness and sanctification and redemption (1 Cor 1).

Section One | On the Gospel

¹⁵He is the image of the invisible God, the firstborn over all creation. ¹⁶ For by Him all things were created that are in heaven and that are on earth, visible and invisible, whether thrones or dominions or principalities or powers. All things were created through Him and for Him. ¹⁷ And He is before all things, and in Him all things consist (Col 1).

³in whom are hidden all the treasures of wisdom and knowledge (Col 2).

¹God, who at various times and in various ways spoke in time past to the fathers by the prophets, ² has in these last days spoken to us by His Son, whom He has appointed heir of all things, through whom also He made the worlds; ³ who being the brightness of His glory and the express image of His person, and upholding all things by the word of His power, when He had by Himself purged our sins, sat down at the right hand of the Majesty on high, ⁴ having become so much better than the angels, as He has by inheritance obtained a more excellent name than they (Heb 1).

Because Jesus Seminar scholars repudiate the Jesus of the New Testament, they allege that the gospels are full of errors. Antagonism against the Jesus of the New Testament is the main presupposition of liberal scholarship. Furthermore, their predisposition against the possibility of miracles prevents them from reading the Bible as history. They also without evidence hypothesize that the lofty words of Christ as recorded in Scripture were actually put in his mouth by Christians from a later time.

A more conservative scholar asks this question, "Can the new Jesus save us?" The answer is "no." The new Jesus of the Jesus seminar is not even interested in saving us. He's not even sure we need saving and, even if we did need saving, this New Jesus has been eviscerated of any divine saving power.

The Jesus Seminar has produced no compelling reasons for Christians to disbelieve these words as spoken by Jesus Christ: "I am the way, the truth, and the life: no one comes to the Father except through me. The Son of Man came to give his life as a ransom for many. Come to me all you who labor and are heavy burdened and I will give you rest."

CHAPTER FIVE

Are All "Faiths" Equal?

All "faiths" are not equal. All "faiths" have an equal right to exist, but not all "faiths" are equal, and not all "faiths" are true. And, if they are not true, they are a lie. There I said it!!

Immediately someone will respond and say that I am a bigot for making that statement, but I think even they know I am simply saying what is obvious to all thinking people. Yes, the modern depraved mind seeks to escape the dilemma of deciding which "faith" is true by redefining truth as "true to me" or "true to you" or "culturally formed truth." But again, in most other areas, the thinking person realizes how silly it is to speak of truth as something that is purely relative. If it is "true to me" without regard to any correspondence to reality, then it is really an illusion.

Illusions may at times be comfortable but eventually a disconnect from reality leads to danger. Is it really safe to build your life and destiny on something that is simply "true to you"? If it's "true to you," but not true to the God "who is truth," can it really be true at all?

I know that is it not politically correct to say another's belief is wrong or that one belief system is better than another, but neither is it intellectually honest or spiritually safe to say that truth only exists in one's mind or it really doesn't matter what you believe.

Why does it matter? I suppose that other "faiths" have answers to that question, but as a Christian here is my response to that question.

- Since there is only one true God, if we worship anyone or anything else, we dishonor Him.

Are All "Faiths" Equal?

- Since the true God has revealed himself as a Trinity (Father-Son-Spirit), if we worship a God who is non-Trinity, we worship an idol, a false god.
- Since this Triune God (Trinity) is our Creator, if we do not worship Him, we rebel against the One to whom our very life belongs.
- Since this God has revealed Himself and His will in creation, history and especially the Holy Bible, if we do not obey Him, we then live as rebels.
- Since this God has planned and accomplished the one way of redemption in Jesus Christ, if we do not submit to Him, we will remain on a path that leads to destruction.
- Since this God's love is so great that His Son, Jesus, would take on human flesh to receive our punishment and die the death that rebels deserve, if we do not trust him, then we will receive punishment and die the death that we deserve.
- Since Jesus is the Son of God, who died, rose again from the dead, lives today, and is coming again to judge and rule the world, if we do not submit to Him as Lord, then we will face Him one day as an enemy, not as a friend.
- Since the one True God offers forgiveness and eternal life as a free gift of His grace to those who submit to Jesus by faith, if we try by any human or religious means to earn God's favor, we insult Him and forfeit any possibility of knowing God's forgiveness and having eternal life.

Now, none of the above matters, if it is not true. But since Jesus rose again from the dead, He is affirmed as the one who is "the truth."

> [30] The times of ignorance God overlooked, but now he commands all people everywhere to repent, [31] because he has fixed a day on which he will judge the world in righteousness by a man whom he has appointed; and of this he has given assurance to all by raising him from the dead (Acts 17).

CHAPTER SIX

The Transcendent Joy of the Gospel

The beginning of the First Epistle of Peter assures us that though we live as exiles of the dispersion, we have been granted a new identity in Christ. In Jesus Christ, we have been granted a new identity that defines us and helps us to live faithfully. A fruit of that identity is that we become a people of a living hope, not despair. Our identity thrives in knowing the value and certainty of what we possess in Christ. But not only do we have a living hope as a fruit of our identity, we have a transcendent joy.

1 Peter 1:6-9 talks about that transcendent joy i.e., one that is experienced in this world but that is not dependent on this world. This joy comes from God the Father, on the basis of the work of Christ, through the ministry of the Holy Spirit in your life.

Because it is a joy that is experienced in being known by Christ and knowing and loving Him and believing His promises, this joy is meant to be the chief joy of our lives, taking priority over all earthly enjoyment.

You may at first say—what in the world are you talking about? What world do you live in? Is it possible that in the midst of suffering, poverty, hatred, loneliness, that one can experience a joy that rises above the trials of life?

If you have not repented of your sins and come to Jesus as the only one who can rescue you, then I understand your skepticism.

However, if you are truly a follower of Jesus Christ, then you have at least tasted of this joy. When you understood the depth of

The Transcendent Joy of the Gospel

your sin and rebellion and the greatness of God's love in rescuing you, in that realization of forgiveness and new life, you experienced a joy that even though everything was not all right in your world,. You became all right (righteous) in God's eyes.

This initial joy of the gospel remains the continuing joy of our lives as we continue to live with a spirit of repentance and dependence upon the gospel of Jesus Christ.

Neither my self-righteousness nor my self-gratification can offer me a transcendent joy; rather they are the chief opponents of the transcendent joy of the gospel.

In Christ I can say: I am chosen, I have a living hope, I now have a transcendent joy. This transcendent joy of the gospel does not eliminate other enjoyment nor does it remove all sorrows, but it does transcend—it stands above all else—untouched by human misery and unrivaled by earthly enjoyment.

CHAPTER SEVEN

Four Cries of the Soul

Years ago I read Kennon Callahan's *Effective Church Leadership*[1] and was struck by what he called the "four foundational searches" of all humanity. He argued that effective leadership understands these searches and seeks to minister to them. The four searches he defined are the search for identity, the search for community, the search for meaning, and the search for hope. In their search for identity, people need to know why they have value, and that they are valued as individuals with their unique personality, gifts, and calling. In their search for community, people need to know they are loved and that they have a necessary contribution to make for the betterment of others. In their search for meaning, people need to know that there is a plausible explanation for the incongruities of life, such as the problem of evil and suffering. And, in their search for hope, people need to know that justice triumphs, righteousness ultimately prevails, and there is a reason to keep on living.

In my experience with people from a variety of cultures, I have found these four searches to be a common thread with all people whether they are post-modern or modern, Eastern or Western, agnostic, skeptic, or believing, young or old, rich or poor. My experience with what I will call "the four cries of the soul" is consistent with the biblical picture of humanity.

The soul cries out in search for the lost identity of being created in the image of God, which essentially consisted of capacity for

---

1. Callahan, *Effective Church Leadership*, 106.

relationship with God. This image, though not erased by human rebellion, is now effaced. The traces of the image which remain initiate the search for a fuller identity, seeking answers to the questions—who am I, from where did I come, why am I here, and where am I going?

Also, the soul cries out for the restoration of the community for which God created humanity. Humanity cannot live fully in isolation but rather longs for a context where one can love and be loved. Originally, when humankind was created (Gen 1:26, 2:18) God determined that humankind should not be a singular lonely being but one sharing likeness to and community with another. Humanity is essentially communal and every soul cries out for this relationship with others.

Additionally, the soul cries out for meaning—an intelligent plausible explanation for the struggles and incongruities of human existences. Everyone lives with the awareness that something is wrong with the world we live in. The soul especially longs for a resolution between a God of compassion, order, justice, and purpose and a world of suffering, disorder, injustice and indifference.

Finally, the soul cries out for hope in the midst of a world of despair. Every soul intuitively knows there must be something better than what is presently experienced and longs for encouraging hope that there is something better.

Now, even though cultures shape both the ways these four searches are understood and the paths these searches take to find fulfillment, ultimately these searches share more commonalties than differences. These four foundational searches are common cries of the human soul. They are the cries of your soul.

As followers of Jesus Christ, we have found that each of these searches finds its resolution in the person and work of Jesus Christ. In his incarnation he exemplifies the ideal human identity as one who knows God and does the will of God. In his life and ministry, especially through the calling of the disciples, he modeled the community that our souls desire. In his crucifixion, he brings the problem of suffering to the forefront and offers us His example of trust in His Father's sovereignty as the ultimate "meaning" for life.

Section One | On the Gospel

In his resurrection, he assures us that there is hope even in and after the most unjust, horrible, tragedies of life.

When we come to Christ in faith, a process of restoring the lost identity is begun and in Him we begin to understand who we really are; in Christ and with his people we begin to experience the community for which our souls cry; in Christ, we begin to realize that our suffering is no less within the Sovereign plan of God than was the suffering of Christ. We are assured by the cross that despite the suffering, disorder, injustice, and indifference in the world, there is a God of order, justice, and purpose; and through the resurrection of Jesus Christ, we are given a new life of hope which is a foretaste of the world to come—a world in which all four foundational searches, i.e., these four cries of the human soul, are fully and finally, forever satisfied.

As followers of Jesus, we seek to minister to others, understanding these four cries of the soul. We minister and lead, as those who hear these cries from our own souls, yet have begun to realize that Jesus hears and responds to those cries. In following him, our longing for identity, community, meaning, and hope is gradually and progressively being satisfied, as we await the ultimate resolution of these cries at His coming.

SECTION TWO

On Theology

CHAPTER EIGHT

Jesus—God's Final and Full Revelation

JESUS: GOD'S FINAL AND FULL REVELATION

Verses 1–3 of Hebrews 1 set the stage for showing us that Jesus fulfills three OT offices of prophet (has spoken). He preaches the prophetic word and he is the Word. He is a superior priest (made purification). He is both the one who makes sacrifice as he is the one, perfect, and acceptable sacrifice for sins. He is also the king (sat down at the right hand of majesty). The priestly element takes center stage in the book of Hebrews.

The Epistles to the Hebrews clarifies the transition from Old Covenant to New Covenant.

Old Covenant Shadows	New Covenant Realties
Law	New Law
Temple	New Temple
Sacrifice	One Sacrifice
High Priests	One High Priest
Priesthood	New Priesthood
Old Covenant	New Covenant
Monarchy	New King
Land	Eternal Kingdom

Section Two | On Theology

In its richness of OT quotations and allusions,[1] Hebrews shows how the Old Testament is about Christ and how that Christ is the fullest and final revelation of God.

Jesus Christ is God's Word for these last days. The Old Testament anticipated and foreshadowed Him, while the NT offers us a full revelation of Him. The following texts remind us that the OT is the word of God about Jesus Christ.

> [25]He said to them, "How foolish you are, and how slow of heart to believe all that the prophets have spoken! [26] Did not the Christ have to suffer these things and then enter his glory?" [27] And beginning with Moses and all the Prophets, he explained to them what was said in all the Scriptures concerning himself (Lk 24).

> [44] He said to them, "This is what I told you while I was still with you: Everything must be fulfilled that is written about me in the Law of Moses, the Prophets and the Psalms." [45] Then he opened their minds so they could understand the Scriptures. [46] He told them, "This is what is written: The Christ will suffer and rise from the dead on the third day, [47] and repentance and forgiveness of sins will be preached in his name to all nations, beginning at Jerusalem (Lk 24).

> [39] You diligently study the Scriptures because you think that by them you possess eternal life. These are the Scriptures that testify about me, [40] yet you refuse to come to me to have life (John 5).

The words of Jesus Christ lead us to conclude that the OT is what we call "progressive, redemptive revelation." It is revelation because in it, God makes himself known. It is redemptive because God reveals himself in the act of redeeming us. It is progressive because God makes himself and his purposes known by stages until the full light is revealed in Jesus Christ.[2]

---

1. When quoting from the Septuagint (Greek translation of OT) the author most often refers to the divine author (God, Christ, Holy Spirit) rather than the human writer. This shows his strong regard for the OT as the Word of God.

2. Goldsworthy, *According to Plan*, 72. Like slowly turning on the dimmer

Jesus—God's Final and Full Revelation

This progressive, redemptive revelation of Jesus Christ is given through historical events, people, promises, institutions, Christophanies, etc., all of which in some way anticipate or foreshadow the final and full revelation in Jesus Christ.

Graeme Goldsworthy sums up the relationship of Jesus Christ to the OT:

> The New Testament emphasizes the historic person of Christ and what he did for us, through faith, to become the friends of God. The emphasis is also on him as the one who sums up and brings to their fitting climax all the promises and expectations raised in the Old Testament. There is a priority of order here, which we must take into account if we are to understand the Bible correctly. It is the gospel event, as that which brings about faith in the people of God, that will motivate, direct, pattern, and empower the life of the Christian community. So we start from the gospel and move to an understanding of Christian living, and the final goal toward which we are moving.
>
> Again, we start from the gospel and move back into the Old Testament to see what lies behind the person and work of Christ. The Old Testament is not completely superseded by the gospel, for that would make it irrelevant to us. It helps us understand the gospel by showing us the origins and meanings of the various ideas and special words used to describe Christ and his works in the New Testament. Yet we must also recognize that Christ is God's fullest and final Word to mankind. As such he reveals to us the final meaning of the Old Testament.[3]

There are many studies that show the relationship of Christ to the Old Testament. An older two-volume study by E.W. Hengstenberg, *Christology of the Old Testament*, was written in 1854. This is a scholarly and detailed study (1400 pages) of Old Testament texts showing the prefiguring and prophecy of Jesus Christ in the Old Testament. A more recent study (1991) by Vern Poythress of Westminster Seminary, *The Shadow of Christ in the Law of Moses*, details

---

in your dining room as images move from darkness to outlines of objects, to shadows, to clear sight.

3. Goldsworthy, *According to Plan*, 83.

how Christ is prefigured in the Pentateuch (5 books of Moses). A look at some of his chapter titles shows how starting with Christ and moving back into the Old Testament gives us insight into a fuller meaning of Christ.

- The Tabernacle of Moses: Prefiguring God's Presence through Christ
- The Sacrifices: Prefiguring the Final Sacrifice of Christ
- The Priests and the People: Prefiguring Christ's Relation to His People
- General Principles for God's Dwelling with Human Beings: Prefiguring Union with Christ.
- The Land of Palestine, the Promised Land: Prefiguring Christ's Renewal and Dominion over the Earth.
- The Law and Its Order: Prefiguring the Righteousness of Christ
- The Purpose of the Tabernacle, the Law, and the Promised Land: Pointing Forward to Christ
- The Punishments and Penalties of the Law: Prefiguring the Destruction of Sin and Guilt Through Christ
- False Worship, Holy War, and Penal Substitution: Prefiguring the Spiritual Warfare of Christ and His Church.[4]

I hope it is clear by now that Jesus Christ is the key to both the Old and New Testaments. We conclude this section with the words of Goldsworthy:

> In order to know how any given part of the Bible relates to us, we must answer two prior questions: how does the text in question relate to Christ, and how do we relate to Christ? Since Christ is the truth, God's final and fullest word to mankind, all other words of the Bible are given their final meaning in him. The same Christ gives us our meaning and defines the significance of our existence in terms of our relationship to him.[5]

---

4. Poythress, *Shadow of Christ*, vii-ix.
5. Goldsworthy, *According to Plan*, 71.

CHAPTER NINE

The Sufficiency of the Word of God

WHY I BELIEVE IN THE SUFFICIENCY OF THE WORD OF GOD AND DIMINISH THE VALUE OF EXTRA-BIBLICAL TRADITION!

1. The Word of God reveals Jesus Christ (John 5:39; Luke 24:25–27, 45–47).
2. The Word of God is the basis of saving faith (John 5:24).
3. The Word of God brings about the new birth (1 Peter 1:23).
4. The Word of God is the truth that sanctifies (John 15:3; 17:17).
5. The Word of God is the ultimate and final standard of judgment (John 12:48).
6. Abiding in the Word of God is evidence of discipleship (John 8:31).
7. The Word of God nourishes our souls (Matthew 4:4; John 6:63; 1 Peter 2:2).
8. The Word of God is sufficient to save and complete us (2 Timothy 3:14–17).
9. We are to make disciples by teaching the Word of God (all which Jesus commanded) (Matthew 28:19–20).
10. Pastors are commanded to preach the Word of God (2 Timothy 4:4)
11. The Word of God endures forever (1 Peter 1:24–25).

Section Two | On Theology

Unverifiable Tradition:

1. There are only three passages in the NT that speak of "apostolic" tradition (1 Corinthians 11:2; 2 Thessalonians 2:15, 3:6).
2. Each of this passages can be taken as teaching that is "passed down."
3. None of these passages indicate any specific tradition that is beyond what is recorded in Scripture.
4. It is unlikely that there would be extra-biblical human tradition when Jesus always condemned tradition that conflicted with the Word of God (Matthew 15:3; Mark 7:8).
5. If there was a tradition in addition to what is revealed in Scripture, it certainly would not replace or contradict the ten statements given above.
6. The church fathers offer no unified witness to any universally accepted tradition apart from Scripture.

CHAPTER TEN

The "Already, Not Yet," Kingdom of Jesus Christ

1. Already a Kingdom in which the King has accomplished redemption through his death and resurrection; not yet a kingdom in which redemption is consummately applied to all things.
2. Already a Kingdom which one sees and enters through repentance and faith; not yet a kingdom which one sees with the physical eye.
3. Already a spiritual kingdom in which the King rules over the hearts and lives of his subjects, not yet, a geo-political kingdom in which all the universe is in subjection to His righteous rule.
4. Already a kingdom in which the subjects of the King are learning to love one another and live in unity; not yet a kingdom in which the subjects of the King perfectly love one another and live in unity.
5. Already a kingdom in which its subjects possess a spiritual inheritance; not yet a kingdom in which the subjects are in full enjoyment of the inheritance.
6. Already a kingdom in which its subjects are granted the New Heavens and Earth; not yet a kingdom in which they possess the New Heavens and Earth.

7. Already a kingdom which is advancing over the powers of darkness; not yet a kingdom which is fully triumphant over the powers of darkness.
8. Already a kingdom in which the power of the King over death, disease, and the devil is evident; not yet a kingdom in which death, disease, and the devil are banished forever.
9. Already a kingdom growing mysteriously and gradually (Matt 13); not yet a kingdom manifested in power and glory.

CHAPTER ELEVEN

Acquiring Knowledge of God

BY WHAT PROCESS DOES MAN ACQUIRE THE KNOWLEDGE OF GOD?

For an accurate knowledge of God we are dependent upon God's self-revelation. Revelation implies a difference between God's knowledge and Man's knowledge. Let me explain by asking and answering a few questions regarding knowledge:

1. What does God know? His knowledge is comprehensive and self-contained. (God never learned anything.)
2. How does God reveal what He knows? God's revelation is both natural and special. Natural revelation is the disclosure of His power and glory in the created universe. Special revelation is the disclosure of His redemptive purposes, primarily through Scripture. In the past special revelation included appearances of God and the incarnation of Jesus Christ.
3. What do men, as creatures, know? Generally, all of his knowledge is limited and derived. He is dependent upon God for knowledge.
4. What can a lost man know?
    a. He can know some things accurately from natural revelation;

      b. He can know nothing completely—he lacks an integrated view that relates all to Christ;

      c. He cannot comprehend some things (special revelation) at all. He doesn't know God.

5. What can a saved man know? He has free access to all of God's revelation, both natural and special.
6. How does a saved man know? Through the two eyes of faith and reason he looks into the room of knowledge. The Spirit of God turns the light on in the room. Through the single lens of the revelation of Jesus Christ everything is brought into proper focus. A lost man has only the single eye of reason, but even that is out of focus, and he peers into a dark room.

There are actually three views of how one can know the truth.[1]

The first view (Secular Humanism) supposes that man is totally independent of a God who either does not exist or who is irrelevant. Man is in control of knowledge that he acquires through his senses and reason. In this view the Bible is just another book without any supernatural character.

The second view (Theistic Humanism) holds that man is only partly independent of God. Man by reason can know the world in which he lives. He depends upon revelation for "religious" knowledge that is added to what he already knows. Francis Schaefer called this a two-story view where faith and reason never intersect. This view has a very weak view of the fall and how the fall has affected Man's thinking. Often in this view human reason stands in judgment on the Bible and decides which revelation to accept or reject.

The third view (Christian Theism) holds that all knowledge is dependent upon God. Since God is Creator of all, all facts are somehow related to God and dependent upon Him for interpretation. This view recognizes that the fall causes all men to suppress the truth and that without regeneration men can never know the truth about God and men will never see any truth in its proper relationship to God.

Goldsworthy offers us five presuppositions that are the underpinnings of our need of special revelation:

---

1. Goldsworthy, *According to Plan*, 45–56.

Acquiring Knowledge of God

1. God made every fact in the universe and He alone can interpret all things and events.
2. Because we are created in the image of God, we know that we are dependent upon God for the truth.
3. As sinners we suppress this knowledge and reinterpret the universe on the assumption that we, not God, give things their meaning.
4. Special revelation through God's redemptive word, reaching its high point in Jesus Christ, is needed to deal with our suppression of the truth and hostility to God.
5. A special work of the Holy Spirit brings repentance and faith so that sinners acknowledge the truth which is in Scripture.[2]

---

2. Goldsworthy, *According to Plan*, 56.

CHAPTER TWELVE

Resurrection Hope

The resurrection of Jesus and the promise of the believer's resurrection offer the ultimate hope in the midst of a world of despair. We are caught between two resurrections—pushed by one in the past and pulled by one in the future. The resurrection of Jesus Christ vindicates His claims to be the Messiah; our future resurrection will ultimately vindicate our faith in Him as the Messiah.

WHAT OUR HOPE IS NOT!

As far as many are concerned, we now live in world without meaning, without promise, without hope—a world of despair. Friedrich Nietzsche (1844-1900), a German philosopher, envisioned that the Western world would collapse into nihilism—the belief that there is no meaning or purpose in existence. Nihilism is the logical consequence of macro evolution.

The first World War terminated Western Europe's faith in modern progress—the anticipation of the promise of a better future.. The dissolution of the Soviet empire canceled faith in Marxism as the guarantee of progress—Marxism's promise of a better world never came to fruition. Though America has been spared the devastations of war and has continued longer in its belief in a better future through modern means, many seem to be accepting the evidence that hope in progress through human means is empty.

Resurrection Hope

Our modern world has not only lost faith in man, but, at the same time, had already declared its independence from God[1], so that there is neither faith in God or faith in man, leaving only faith in nothing, or faith in faith, both of which lead to despair and disappointment.

Nietzsche was partially correct as Robert Jenson points out, when he predicted that "There would at once appear the hollow "last man" and the glorious "superman." The hollow "last man" is clearly on the seen, but the glorious "superman" is so far missing."[2]

In this world of despair, many are the spiritual entrepreneurs who generate salvation programs to offer hope. One such program is that of Maharishi Mahesh Yogi. "If, says Yogi, a sufficient number of people led by trained mediators could be induced to sit still and meditate for ninety minutes each morning and evening, the positive waves they emitted would ensure universal peace, improved economy, and a reduction of the crime rate, to say nothing of the physical and spiritual well-being of one and all. The cost to employ seven thousand mediators would be $20 million . . . ."[3] Despair often becomes desperate. That desperation is seen in the proliferation of New Age, Eastern religion, cults, etc.

Biblical hope is not merely the promise of a better world. Biblical hope does not guarantee an immediate solution to all the present crises of life. Biblical hope does not exempt us from present suffering. Biblical hope does not believe that modernism, human reasoning, education, government, liberal programs, etc. insure progress in the world.

Remember the men on the road to Emmaus after Jesus died and before they knew he was alive:

> ²¹But we were hoping that it was He who was going to redeem Israel. Indeed, besides all this, it is the third day since these things happened (Lk 24).

---

1. "Modernism is the condition that begins when humans understand that God is really dead and that they therefore have to decide all the big questions for themselves." Jenson, *First Things*, 19.
2. Jenson, *First Things*, 19.
3. Sisk, *First Things*, 9.

Proverbs 13:12 says: "Hope deferred makes the heart sick, But desire fulfilled is a tree of life."

WHAT IS OUR HOPE?

Our hope is a promise from God based on an historical event, tied to the prophetic word of the living God, and connected to a future event. Essentially, the gospel is a historical, personal, and eschatological message. Our hope is in a person, Jesus Christ, and all the events, both past, present, and future, that involve that person.

How do we address a world of despair? Is there an anchor for that life which appears to be no more than a small cork drifting on the vast and unpredictable ocean waters? Yes, Jesus, who died for sinners, has risen from the grave and offers new life, eternal life, to all who will find their life in Him.

Actually, the world of despair in which we live offers the church of Jesus Christ a fresh opportunity—an opportunity we will lose if we fail to be "the sweet aroma of the knowledge of Him in every place" (2 Cor. 2:14, see 14–17). Because as Heb. 6:18-19 reminds us ". . . we may have strong encouragement, we who have fled for refuge in laying hold of the hope set before us. This hope we have as an anchor of the soul, a hope both sure and steadfast . . . ."

Foundational to the Christian hope is belief in the historical (time/space) resurrection of Jesus Christ. Jesus lives. Because He lives, we live also—not only here and now, but forever with Him. His resurrection not only vindicates His claims but assures us that "life" is more than what we presently experience. Whatever may be your lot in this temporal world—this world is not the end. That same Jesus who conquered sin, death, and Satan through His death at the cross is RISEN and, because He lives, we live with Him—FOREVER!

CHAPTER THIRTEEN

The Human Condition

The Bible does not offer a definitive explanation of how evil entered the universe. We know from the Bible that Satan, a created being, is evil and that he existed prior to the fall of man. Scriptures do not explain how Satan became evil. They simply present him as evil and as God's opponent as he enters the stage in the drama of human life.

Satan's method of deceit in the Garden of Eden brings about the fall of humanity and sets the pattern for all future deceptions. In the temptation (Genesis 3:1–5) Satan entices Eve to eat of the forbidden Tree of the Knowledge of good and evil. God had set this test so that Adam and Eve would experience moral discernment at the highest level of obedience.

Satan asserted doubt concerning God's ways and he attacked God's character by implying that God was unfair in not giving Adam and Eve access to every tree. He focused on the negative prohibition. Eve succumbed to Satan's wiles. She misquoted God's permission, God's prohibition, and God's penalty. She made the fatal mistake of not being careful with the Word of God.

Satan responded by blatantly denying God's word. Satan essentially said:

1. You won't reap what you sow;
2. God fears, rather than loves man;
3. You can be independent of God;
4. There is efficacy in things;

5. Don't trust God's Word.

Satan propagates these same lies today. Satan succeeded in taking Eve's focus from God to self. Now that God is questioned, she trusts her own reasoning and Eve acts by sight rather than by faith. She sees; she covets; she takes; she draws others (Adam) into sin. The consequences of sin (3:7–12) are separation, alienation, and anguish. There had been harmony between God and man; man and man; man and animals; man and land. Now all harmony is gone as God's word and order are violated. The woman listens to Satan, the man listens to the woman, and then the man attempts to have God listen to him.

Every human is infected by the sin of the parents of the human race. As Romans 5:12 states: "Therefore, just as sin entered the world through one man, and death through sin, and in this way death came to all men, because all sinned."

From the fall of humanity on, all future history and revelation is redemptive in nature. The effects of sin are so pervasive and powerful that only a divine solution will suffice. When you move from the fall in Genesis 3 to chapter 4, you immediately realize that sin has passed from parent to child. The story of Cain and Able is not told to warn us of the dangers of jealousy and hatred. Rather it shows the solidarity of the human race in Adam's sin (Romans 5:12–21); sin has been passed on to the next generation. Moreover, it demonstrates the alienation between an individual, his brother, and his God.

The pervasive and powerful effects of sin as revealed in the history of Genesis 4–11 prepare us for God's sovereign intervention in the call of Abraham and the series of Old Testament covenants that anticipate the death and resurrection of Jesus Christ, God's only solution for sin. All the distortions of God's created order are ultimately restored through God's Anointed, Jesus Christ. The complete restoration awaits the Second Coming of Christ when sin and its effects will be removed (2 Peter 3:10–13; Revelation 21:1–5).

CHAPTER FOURTEEN

Unity, Despite Theological Difference

I love theological reflection—trying to determine the correct meaning of biblical texts and what they teach us about God, ourselves, and the world we live in. I love theological formulation—attempting to classify and arrange theological affirmations in a systematic form. I love theological interaction—discussing with those who also reflect and formulate, yet who often come to different affirmations.

I believe that theological reflection, formulation, and interaction are healthy for the believer and the church and that they serve to refine one's understanding of what biblical texts say about what God has done, is doing and will ultimately do in this world and the world to come. The process of theological reflection, formulation, and interaction also serves to restrain the tendency to elevate our isolated, contextually limited understanding of Scripture.

Theological reflection, formulation, and interaction should ultimately result in a greater transformation of life and ministry.

> [16] All Scripture is breathed out by God and profitable for teaching, for reproof, for correction, and for training in righteousness, [17] that the man of God may be competent, equipped for every good work (2 Tim).

However, I've observed that in order for the process of theological reflection, formulation, and interaction to be profitable instead of divisive, it needs to take place within certain parameters that insure that Christian unity is preserved. Those parameters, I suggest are as follows:

- The foundation of relationship with my brothers and sisters in Christ of our common understanding of and shared experience in the gospel of Jesus Christ is the meeting point for theological reflection, formulation, and interaction.

- The self-evident, axiomatic, and perspicuous theology of the gospel of Jesus Christ undergirds the theological enterprise.

    [16] For God so loved the world, that he gave his only Son, that whoever believes in him should not perish but have eternal life. [17] For God did not send his Son into the world to condemn the world, but in order that the world might be saved through him. [18] Whoever believes in him is not condemned, but whoever does not believe is condemned already, because he has not believed in the name of the only Son of God (John 3).

    [3] For I delivered to you as of first importance what I also received: that Christ died for our sins in accordance with the Scriptures, [4] that he was buried, that he was raised on the third day in accordance with the Scriptures (1 Cor 15).

    [30] Jesus did many other signs in the presence of the disciples, which are not written in this book; [31] but these are written so that you may believe that Jesus is the Christ, the Son of God, and that by believing you may have life in his name (John 20).

- The New Commandment of Jesus and the intercessory prayer of Jesus for unity are to be preserved at all costs as we engage in the theological enterprise.

    [34] A new commandment I give to you, that you love one another: just as I have loved you, you also are to love one another. [35] By this all people will know that you are my disciples, if you have love for one another (John 13).

Unity, Despite Theological Difference

> [20] I do not ask for these only, but also for those who will believe in me through their word, [21] that they may all be one, just as you, Father, are in me, and I in you, that they also may be in us, so that the world may believe that you have sent me. [22] The glory that you have given me I have given to them, that they may be one even as we are one, [23] I in them and you in me, that they may become perfectly one, so that the world may know that you sent me and loved them even as you loved me (John 17).

- A shared commitment to inerrancy and biblical authority undergird all of our reflection, formulation, and interaction with Scripture.

  > Now these Jews were more noble than those in Thessalonica; they received the word with all eagerness, examining the Scriptures daily to see if these things were so (Acts 17:11)

  > [19] And we have something more sure, the prophetic word, to which you will do well to pay attention as to a lamp shining in a dark place, until the day dawns and the morning star rises in your hearts, [20] knowing this first of all, that no prophecy of Scripture comes from someone's own interpretation. [21] For no prophecy was ever produced by the will of man, but men spoke from God as they were carried along by the Holy Spirit (2 Pet).

- Councils, creeds, and confessions should have only a tertiary, non-authoritative role in the understanding of Scripture.

  > [6] And he said to them, "Well did Isaiah prophesy of you hypocrites, as it is written, "'This people honors me with their lips, but their heart is far from me; [7] in vain do they worship me, teaching as doctrines the commandments of men.' [8] You leave the commandment of God and hold to the tradition of men." [9] ¶ And he said to them, "You

have a fine way of rejecting the commandment of God in order to establish your tradition (Mark 7).

- Engagement in theological reflection, formulation, and interaction intends to move beyond the theoretical and answer the question of how life and ministry are transformed.

> [32] And now I commend you to God and to the word of his grace, which is able to build you up and to give you the inheritance among all those who are sanctified (Acts 20).

> [4] For whatever was written in former days was written for our instruction, that through endurance and through the encouragement of the Scriptures we might have hope. [5] May the God of endurance and encouragement grant you to live in such harmony with one another, in accord with Christ Jesus, [6] that together you may with one voice glorify the God and Father of our Lord Jesus Christ (Rom 15).

> [1] Paul, a servant of Christ Jesus, called to be an apostle, set apart for the gospel of God, [2] which he promised beforehand through his prophets in the holy Scriptures, [3] concerning his Son, who was descended from David according to the flesh [4] and was declared to be the Son of God in power according to the Spirit of holiness by his resurrection from the dead, Jesus Christ our Lord, [5] through whom we have received grace and apostleship to bring about the obedience of faith for the sake of his name among all the nations, [6] including you who are called to belong to Jesus Christ (Romans 1).

These five parameters provide a starting point for theological reflection, formulation, and interaction within the body of Christ. A process that will be gracious and non-divisive. These parameters invite charismatics and cessationists, Calvinists and non-Calvinists, dispensationalists and covenant theologians and new covenant theologians, those who abstain and those who imbibe, and all those who find they do not quite fit into neat categories.

Unity, Despite Theological Difference

In the context of gospel-centeredness, biblical love and unity, commitment to Scripture, rejection of man-made authorities, and passion to grow and reach out, the enterprise of theological reflection, formulation, and interaction will yield the fruit of glory to God, peace among the people of God, and greater impact on the nations.

CHAPTER FIFTEEN

The Continuity of Theological Concepts

A NEW COVENANT READING OF OLD COVENANT TEXTS

While studying and teaching Zechariah 9–14 near Beirut, Lebanon I was challenged to think about the meaning and relevance of those chapters to Lebanese believers who often suffer because of the animosity between Lebanon and the very nation and people who are mentioned in those chapters. Does an alleged promised restoration of Israel and Jerusalem bring comfort or chagrin to believers in Lebanon? After all, are not Arabic speaking believers and Jewish believers in the Middle East the true people of God? Are they not the ones who should expect to share in the triumph of God? Does present day Israel have a "favored nation" status that trumps the "holy nation" of the church (1 Pet 2:9–10)? Furthermore, does not a similar conundrum exist for those of us who live in North America? Do these texts have anything relevant to say to a largely Gentile church? Do we simply rejoice because ethnic Israel is to be restored or do we rejoice because the triumph which the old covenant nation expected is the triumph that belongs to all of those who are children of God through faith in Jesus Christ? Admittedly, the question of relevancy should not be determinative

The Continuity of Theological Concepts

in the understanding of biblical texts but it does raise questions that might not be raised otherwise.

Additionally, not only does the difficulty of finding relevance in Zechariah 9–14 to Lebanese and North American believers pose a challenge, but so does a careful reading of the New Testament. Reading the Old and New Testaments separately, one might conclude that two distinct and contrasting bibles exist (Old Testament and New Testament) written to two distinct peoples (Jews and Christians) with only shared lessons of moral application or common interest in the promised Messiah. Otherwise, one might conclude that God has distinct purposes for Jews and Gentiles. While interpreting texts in isolation from the larger corpus of Scripture makes this conclusion textually possible, a canonical reading of the Bible questions whether it is theologically justifiable and whether it adequately represents the biblical-theological message of the Bible which centers in the restoration of God's original purposes as presented in Genesis 1–2, distorted in Genesis 3–11, given new hope in Genesis 12, and consummated in the coming of the Messiah.

Admittedly, a "pre-New Testament" reading of Zechariah 9–14 and the Old Testament on its own may lead one to conclude that ethnic Israelites are the people of God, earthly Jerusalem is the city He has chosen, He is present in the Jewish temple, the enemies of Israel will be defeated and Gentiles will make their way to Jerusalem, the Messiah will come humbly on a donkey and in glory with a display of power, etc.

However, Christians cannot read the Old Testament on its own because it is not on its own. It is part of the Christian Bible which includes both Old and New Testament. The Old Testament is a book of introduction, preparation, and expectation; the New Testament is a book of conclusion, denouement, and fulfillment. The OT informs the NT by giving background, promises, and a developing story line. The NT finalizes the story line and sees promise come to fulfillment.

The OT helps us understand the NT by introducing theological concepts which are continued in the NT, such as God, creation, sin, redemption, kingdom, people of God, temple, holy city, enemies, exile and restoration, etc. The NT expands on these concepts

49

often giving them new clarity in light of the full and final revelation that comes with the advent of Jesus Christ.

Though there is continuity of theological concepts, there is discontinuity in the contextualization of these concepts. I suggest that in both the Old and New Testaments God addresses his people in language and terms that they generally understood, yet retaining a bit of mystery, because the ultimate reality, which God brings in the triumph of the Messiah, defies the ability of human language to fully convey.

If in the future believing Jews of the old covenant see the New Jerusalem coming out of heaven and witness the triumph of God over all evil and enemies, would they say, "I'm disappointed that it did not turn out "literally" as portrayed in the language of the OT." No, they would likely say, "This fulfillment not only satisfies all which God promised but goes far beyond what could be expected. Thank you, Lord."

As I read Zechariah 9–14 and similar texts in light of the New Testament I look for theological concepts that are continuous between the testaments and interpret them in light of the fuller and final revelation of the New Testament. For instance, the theological theme of "people of God" is represented primarily by Israel in the Old Testament. Yet, we understand in the New Testament that the true "seed" of Abraham were those who had the faith of Abraham, regardless of ethnicity (Rom 2; Gal 3; 1 Pet 2). The "holy city" of the Old Testament was physical, geographical Jerusalem; in the New Testament the holy city is the New Jerusalem (Heb 12:18–24, Rev 21, 22). Furthermore, the New Testament even suggests that Abraham knew that the physical reality of "land and city" anticipated something more than earthly geography (Heb 11:10, 16; Rom 4:13). The theme of "temple as the place of God's presence" in the Old Testament was primarily confined to the tabernacle and temple of ancient Israel; in the New Testament, Jesus is ultimately the temple (John 2:19—destroy this temple), believers and the church are the temple (1 Cor 3:16; 6:19), and there is no need of a temple in the new order because God's presence pervades everything (Rev 21:3, 22).

The Continuity of Theological Concepts

There are other shared themes such as the ultimate triumph of God, the defeat of enemies, the removal of sin, the transformation of nature, the restoration of the cosmos, the establishment of worship and holiness. In Zechariah 9–14 all of these concepts are portrayed in old covenant language at times exceeding the limits of that language, anticipating the inauguration of the greater realities of the New Covenant and ultimately the consummation.

Old Testament saints had a "two-age" view of history—the age in which they lived and the age to come. The age to come anticipated the advent of the Messiah and the Day of the Lord in which God's people would be delivered and His enemies would be judged. The age to come was depicted in terms that related to the age in which they lived though the seed of old covenant concepts blossoms into the unforeseen beauty of new covenant realities.

The New Testament declares that "the age to come" was inaugurated at the first advent of Christ (Lk 1:67–80; Acts 2:29–36), that we live in the age that was anticipated (1 Cor 10:11—"on whom the end of the ages has come"), but, though the age has *already* come, it is *not yet* consummated, so we anticipate the consummation at His Second Advent (2 Thess 1:5–10).

Consequently, New Covenant believers live between two worlds: having entered the kingdom (Col 1:13) but waiting for the consummate kingdom (Rev 11:15); having become part of the new creation (2 Cor 5:17), yet waiting for the consummate new creation (Rev 21); being seated in the heavens with Christ (Eph 2:6), yet living as strangers on earth (1 Pet 2:11); having witnessed the triumph of Christ over sin, Satan, and death (Col 1:13–15), yet awaiting the consummate world of righteousness (2 Pet 3:13); having tasted in the Spirit the inheritance to come (Eph 1:13–14), yet awaiting consummate glory (1 Pet 5:1).

CHAPTER SIXTEEN
God: The Perfect Theologian

Perfect knowledge resides only in God. God is infinite; His knowledge is infinite. Because man is finite, his knowledge is finite.

Because God's knowledge is perfect and complete, there is an ultimate rationality to the universe, contrary to the ultimate irrationality of modern thought.

Because God's knowledge of Himself is complete, it is also systematic. Because it is systematic, systematic theology and systematic study of the universe is possible. A belief in the randomness of the universe renders impossible the systematic study of the world.

Man is created with capacity to know God and His world. Being made in the image of God, there is a similarity, not identity, of personality that endows man with this capacity. The entrance of sin effaced this capacity, but did not erase it. The work of the Spirit in regeneration is to restore this effacement.

Man's creation by God establishes two levels of existence, God's and man's. God's existence is self-contained, while man's existence is derivative.[1] For this reason there must be two levels of knowledge, God's and man's. God's knowledge is complete and self-contained, while man's knowledge is "derivative and re-interpretive."[2]

---

1. Van Til, *Systematic Theology*, 12.
2. Van Til, *Systematic Theology*, 12.

God: The Perfect Theologian

> As man's existence is dependent upon an act of voluntary creation on the part of God, so man's knowledge depends upon an act of voluntary revelation of God to man.[3]

All human knowledge depends on "an original act of creation and revelation on the part of the self-existent God of Scripture."[4]

God's knowledge of Himself is complete and can never be added to. Man's knowledge of God is incomplete and subject to corrections and addition. Human theologians are always in the process of developing theology. Man's knowledge of God can be accurate, but not perfect. And, even that sense of accuracy is held tentatively. This knowledge of the tentativeness of our theological statements breeds humility, as we continue to study God's revelation.

God's knowledge of the world is also complete. His knowledge is instant, not progressive. God's knowledge of the world has never been added to. God has never learned anything new about the world. Man's knowledge of the world is incomplete and subject to correction and addition. Science is a progressive study. Findings may be accurate, but not perfect. Even accurate findings are held tentatively, not absolutely.

Though both regenerate and unregenerate men may discover the "facts" of this world, only regenerate men may rightly interpret those facts. The interpretation of facts is not dependent on reason, but on revelation. The Scriptures speak to all of life whether directly of indirectly.

God's Word revelation is complete and perfect. It is sufficient for this life and needs no addition or correction. It alone addresses matters with absoluteness. The tentativeness of our interpretations does not detract from the absoluteness of its revelation. Our interpretations may be accurate, but never perfect. They may be held firmly, but not absolutely. They are held with humility, being willing to allow further study to correct and enhance.

If God is good and not evil, and only God is eternal, then evil cannot be eternal. It must be created and controlled by God.

---

3. Van Til, *Systematic Theology*, 12.
4. Van Til, *Systematic Theology*, 13.

Section Two | On Theology

The world apart from Christ has access only to one channel of God's revelation—the natural world. However, its interpretation of that is distorted.

Because of the unity of God's revelation (natural and special) based upon the unity inherent in the nature of God, wisdom living cannot be attained without a knowledge of both. The Word of God is not learned in a vacuum, and the natural world needs to be informed by the Word of God.

CHAPTER SEVENTEEN

Divine Sovereignty and Human Freedom

While pastoring in Queens I was asked to teach on six questions presented to me, which came out of their discussion on the Westminster Catechism. I would love to be able to tell you that I was or am prepared to answer their questions definitively so that there would be no further questions. Unfortunately (or providentially, depending in how you view God's Sovereignty), I will not say enough that will bring anyone's mind to rest on this subject.

The questions presented to me were as follows:

1. When it says Jesus died for all, what does "all" represent
2. What happens in the heart of man when he becomes saved?
3. Is it true that the Holy Spirit knocks at the heart and we decide whether or not to accept?
4. Can we resist, or say no to the Holy Spirit?
5. Who controls the born-again process? man? God?
6. If God didn't give us a choice to choose him, wouldn't we all be robots?

As I perused the questions, I realized that questions 3–6 are really nuances of one question regarding the relationship of God's Sovereignty and Human Responsibility (Free will). The other two questions can stand alone, but they also are related to the discussion of God's Sovereignty and Human Responsibility.

Section Two | On Theology

I will briefly answer the first two questions then deal more extensively with Questions #3–6.

QUESTION #1—WHEN IT SAYS JESUS DIED FOR ALL, WHAT DOES "ALL" REPRESENT?

Many of those who hold strongly to God's Sovereignty (Calvinism) answer Question #1 by saying that "all" means "all the elect, i.e. those whom God chose before the foundation of the world."

Those who hold most strongly to "Human Responsibility" (Arminianism) answer Question #1 saying that "all" means "all human beings in every time and place." In between these views are various nuances of what "all" means. Admittedly, there are verses in Scripture where "all" is defined by the immediate context and does not necessarily mean "everyone in the world." For instance, listen to Romans 8:32,

> He who did not spare his own Son but gave him up for us all, how will he not also with him graciously give us all things?

Here the "all" for whom Christ was given and who receive "all things" are certainly not every individual in the world who receive everything that is in the world. The context text tells us here that Christ gave himself for those to whom Paul is writing (but not only those) and will give them all things that are purchased and promised in the death of Christ.

There are other times where "all" means "all the world," such as in 2 Corinthians 5:14–15,

> [14] For the love of Christ controls us, because we have concluded this: that one has died for all, therefore all have died; [15] and he died for all, that those who live might no longer live for themselves but for him who for their sake died and was raised.

In this text Christ death is for all because all are dead in trespasses and sin (Eph 2:1). Those who do come to life benefit in a particular way from the death and resurrection of Christ and have a redefined purpose for their lives, i.e., "to live for him."

When we talk about the extent of the atonement (i.e., for whom did Christ die?), we need to consider the issues of sufficiency (value) and efficacy (accomplishment). Verses such as John 3:16 and 1 John 2:2 speak of sufficiency; verses such as Eph 5:25; Matt 1:21; Mark 10:45, speak of efficacy.

At the end of any discussion on the extent of the atonement, all evangelicals believe that the atonement is limited in some sense. Unless you are a Universalist, you do not believe that the death of Christ effects or secures the redemption of all men in every place. I prefer the formulation "sufficient for all; efficient for the elect (or those who believe)."

QUESTION #2 — WHAT HAPPENS IN THE HEART OF MAN WHEN HE BECOMES SAVED?

A new life is planted within by the presence of the Holy Spirit so that now one's disposition (nature) is toward God (2 Cor 5:17; 2 Peter 1:3-4) instead of in rebellion against God (Rom 3:10-12), though the vestiges (traces) of sin yet remain in his being. Some would say that this takes place prior to faith, some say after faith, and others coordinate regeneration with faith. Whatever we call the work of the Spirit prior to faith (conviction, prevenient grace, regeneration), all evangelicals believe that there is a necessary work of the Spirit to enable faith to occur.

The more difficult question is "do all men equally experience this work of the Spirit that brings them to salvation?" The obvious answer is no. Calvinists, noting this reality, distinguish between a general call and an efficacious call. Arminians believe that there is a "prevenient grace" for all men which some resist. The answer to why some receive an efficacious call (Calvinism) and some resist or respond to prevenient grace (Arminianism) is an answer that includes both God's Sovereignty and Human Responsibility leaving us with what J. I. Packer calls an "antinomy."[1]

1. In philosophy, contradiction, real or apparent, between two principles

Section Two | On Theology

QUESTIONS #3-6

Now let us consider questions 3-6. I empathize with the consternation evidenced by these questions because over the years of my being in Christ, I have wrestled time and again with the relationship of God's Sovereignty and Human Responsibility. When I reflect on this relationship I do so from various perspectives. I consider myself to be a Christian, a pastor, a biblical theologian, and an evangelist. In each of those roles I find that the answer to the question reflects a similar balance, or someone might say, imbalance. Both Arminians and Calvinists have their systems and their exegesis of texts that support their systems. We could go over the myriad of texts that are debated on this subject, but the truth is that our predisposition to a doctrinal system or way of thinking theologically bears great influence on how we understand those texts.

Therefore, what I choose to do is to talk a little about how I think about these issues from the perspectives of a Christian, a pastor, a biblical theologian, and an evangelist.

As a Christian, I marvel at why I become a recipient of God's grace. Even though I know that my repentance and faith were genuinely my choice, I wonder why I made that choice, and others who had equal opportunity did not make that choice, and why some died without ever having an opportunity. I can only conclude that my salvation has more to do with God's sovereignty and less with my own power of choice and certainly not the goodness of my heart. However, my choice was really "my" choice. I also find great assurance in knowing that I am kept by the power of a Sovereign God and am not dependent on my freedom of will to remain in Christ forever. Though my will is active both in salvation and sanctification, I depend on the "God who works in you, both to will and to work for his good pleasure" (Phil 2:13).

As a pastor, I have found that at some point everyone wants to and needs to believe in God's Sovereignty. What Christian doesn't want a sovereign and powerful God to bring loved ones and friends to himself? Who doesn't want to believe that "God is working all

---

or conclusions, both of which seem equally justified—http://www.britannica.com/eb/article-9007849/antinomy.

Divine Sovereignty and Human Freedom

things for the good of those who love him and are called according to his purpose?" Who doesn't want a God who sovereignly brings to pass all that he has purposed for us in Jesus Christ? Yet, the Bible also calls people to accept responsibility for their choices and the consequences of their decisions for right and wrong. I believe in both God's Sovereignty and Human responsibility, but in those intensely critical moments of life, I find more comfort in the sovereignty of God than in the freedom of human choice.

As a biblical theologian, I have wrestled with the problem/challenge of making the exegesis of biblical texts conform consistently to theological systems. As a young Christian, when I was unaware of Calvinism/Aminianism, I was quite comfortable living with the seeming contradictions, mysteries, and ambiguities of Scripture, simply taking Scripture as I found it. Marriage to a theological system, as well as the influence of Western thought processes (i.e. the rationalism of the modern age), cause one to work for logical consistency in exegesis. Often this leads to a "stretched" interpretation of texts that don't neatly fit the system. Perhaps, an example of this is that Calvin seemed to be more of a Calvinist in his Institutes of Christian Religion and less of one in his biblical commentaries. I personally find that Calvinists (Reformed theologians) do better with biblical exegesis and theological formations than others do. This isn't to say that there are nor good Arminian theologians, such as I. Howard Marshall and Roger E. Olson . There just are not that many of them. I find Reformed theologians more coherent, even though at times I believe they are bending a text to fit their system. Though I personally do not like the labels (Calvinist or Arminian), if I had a gun to my head, I would reluctantly choose Calvinism, even though some Calvinists might think I'm more Arminian. Either way, I have no desire to be a flag-waving, card-carrying Calvinist. My Calvinistic leanings are just that "leanings." They are not solid, bedrock convictions, but leanings and tendencies that gravitate more toward God's Sovereignty.

When it comes to the doctrine of predestination, though Calvinists and Arminians differ in the logical order of God's decrees, they both end up with a God who creates a world in which he knows from the beginning that some will come to Christ and others will go to hell. Whether this occurs because He sovereignly ordained this outcome on the basis of his good pleasure or he ordained this outcome on basis of knowing beforehand who would believe, the outcome remains the same, i.e. God created a world in which he knew what the outcome would be.

I've often mentally wrestled with the relationship of God's omniscience to his decrees. Does he know things because they will happen or do things happen because his knowing is equal to ordaining? I understand that all events are *certain* from God's perspective. Certainty has to do with the "factness of the event." I deduce from the Bible that some certain events are *necessary*, i.e. God has declared and caused the event to be (Isa 42:9), and some certain events are *contingent*, involving the free acts of moral agents where the event could go more than one way (i.e. should I choose life or death) (Deut 30:19), but which way it will go God knows. Also, some certain events include elements of both necessity and contingency (Acts 2:23). When it comes to the sinner's choice to repent and believe, does true contingency exist? Since one's will is bound and determined by his nature, and a sinner's nature is in rebellion and rejection of God, does true contingency exist in one's choice for salvation? If left to contingency alone, would a free moral agent would ever come to Christ one his own? I think not—"no one seeks after God." Though Calvinists (regeneration before faith) and Arminians (Prevenient grace) differ as to the work of the Spirit necessary for one to believe, they both believe that men dead in their sins depend upon a work of God's grace to enable true faith to occur.

As an evangelist, I am much more of a Calvinist when praying for the lost. My confidence in the success of the gospel is in the power of the Spirit to bring unwilling sinners to a willingness to come to Christ. I do want a sovereign God to open eyes blinded by Satan and to bring dead men to life. I have no hope in the freedom of the human will to heal one's own blindness or to resurrect oneself. I do not need a strong view of particular redemption in order to hold this view of God's Sovereign power, i.e., my belief that God can and does powerfully bring people to himself is not necessitated by the belief that Jesus died only for those people. On the other hand, I may appear more Arminian in the practice of evangelism. I make strong

Divine Sovereignty and Human Freedom

appeal to everyone's responsibility to hear, repent, and believe. I do believe in the "possibility" that anyone can be saved, though I know the "actuality" is that "the gate is straight and narrow and there are few who find it." Why do some enter that gate? Yes, some find it and choose to enter. But why does one choose and another remains on the broad way to destruction? Is there something better or nobler in one sinner than in another that enables him to choose? Or, is there something within the eternal plan of God that enables one to choose while not enabling another? Herein, I live with a conundrum. I would like to believe that the answer lies somewhere in between, unrecognizable by my finite mind. Though I lean more toward God's Sovereignty, because of what I know from the Bible about human depravity, I also believe in resistible and irresistible grace. There are instances where people resist the Spirit's call and there are instances where others are overwhelmed by the Spirit's call. What makes the difference? Again, that is the conundrum, the mystery I live with. I agree with Albert Mohler when he says,

> I mentioned there are two impossible persons. First is the person that does not desire Christ who is irresistibly drawn to Him. And the second person that does not exist is the person who wishes to respond to faith in Christ but is denied his faith—in other words, those who would call upon the name of the Lord and be denied.[2]

I believe this is God's world with His plan and purpose. We may wrestle and differ with how human responsibility fits into that world, nevertheless, "the earth is the Lord's and the fullness of it, the world, and they who dwell in it." If you are in a chess game in which your opponent is a master of strategy who knows all your options and choices and has such a thorough plan that influences and counteracts your every move, ensuring the outcome—you may enjoy the game, your moves will reflect your real choices, but you will not win unless he lets you win.

In the following diagram, I would place myself a little left of center, though a hyper-Calvinist might say I am far right of center and an Arminian might say I'm far left of center.

2. Mohler, 2006 Pastors Conference.

Section Two | On Theology

Calvinism		Arminianism	
More Sovereignty of God		*Less Sovereignty of God*	
5 ————4————3————2—JPD-	1 ——1	————2————3————4————5	
Less Responsibility of Man		*More Responsibility of Man*	
Total Depravity		Human Ability	
Unconditional Election		Conditional Election	
Limited Atonement		Unlimited Atonement	
Irresistible Grace		Resistible Grace	
Perseverance of the Saints		Conditional Secuirty	

CONCLUSIONS

1. The Bible teaches both the Sovereignty of God and the Responsibility of man.

   [11] In him we have obtained an inheritance, having been predestined according to the purpose of him who works all things according to the counsel of his will (Eph 1).

   [13] For everyone who calls on the name of the Lord will be saved (Rom 10).

2. The two major theological systems mainly differ on how they understand the relationship between and their emphasis on the Sovereignty of God and the Responsibility of man.

   Calvinism:
   Election based on God's free and sovereign choice.

   Arminianism:
   Election Based on (fore) knowledge—God elected those whom He knew would of their own free will believe in Christ and persevere in the faith.

Divine Sovereignty and Human Freedom

3. Any theological system that denies either the Sovereignty of God or the Responsibility of man is an errant system. (hyper-Calvinism and Pelagianism)[3]
4. Any theological system that assumes they have completely resolved all the philosophical, theological, and exegetical issues in reconciling the Sovereignty of God and the Responsibility of man is an arrogant system.
5. Every theological system is man-made and, though some may be more adequate and coherent than others, no system perfectly harmonizes the full content of Scripture. My conclusion is that Reformed theology does a more adequate job and is more coherent.
6. The essentials of Christianity are not defined by a system; neither is the unity of believers based on agreement on how the issues of Divine Sovereignty and Human Responsibility are worked out. Both Calvinists and Arminians agree on the Five *solas* of the Reformation—*the Bible alone, by grace alone, through faith alone, in Christ alone, to the glory of God alone.* Let us love one another on the basis of these. Heaven is populated by those who confess Jesus as Lord regardless of how they understand how they came to that confession.
7. Though looking for greater precision in theology is important, our priority should always be obedience to our commission to preach the gospel and make disciples of all nations.

---

3. "Pelagius taught that a person is born with the same purity and moral abilities as Adam was when he was first made by God. He taught that people can choose God by the exercise of their free will and rational thought. God's grace, then, is merely an aid to help individuals come to Him." Slick, *Pelagianism*.

CHAPTER EIGHTEEN

Calvinism on the "N" Train

As I sat on the "N" train this morning[1], I looked into the face of a Chinese man, old, tired, and alone. I wondered, "if Calvinism is true, is this man one of the ones God loved enough to send his Son to die or is this man excluded from any possibility of grace. Does God care about this man or is he one who is not the object of God's love?" What a troubling thought!

I continued to look at this lonely man across the aisle and thought about the apparent contradiction between Calvinism and encountering real people on the "N" train from Brooklyn to Queens: I asked myself: "Is God most glorified by the expression of His great love for all or by the expression of His sovereign power in electing and predestining a few? Why is that grace must be irresistible for a chosen few? Is the love, goodness, and grace of God in the

---

1. The N Train runs from Coney Island in Brooklyn to Astoria in Queens, taking the long route as an express train through Manhattan. Half the time it runs above ground including views of Brooklyn, Queens, and Manhattan as it travels across the Manhattan Bridge, and views of Astoria and Long Island City running through Queens. The route of the N Train captures the ethnic diversity of the city as it winds through Russian, Hasidic, Chinese, Italian, Hispanic, Middle Eastern, and other neighborhoods. The economic diversity of the city is also reflected in its path as it stops in a lower income area like Sunset Park, among a flurry of small businesses in Chinatown, or at the upscale stores of both 5th Avenue and Lexington Ave. If you love to eat, then you can enjoy the cuisines of the world starting with borsch in Coney Island, ending with Fried Kefalotiri cheese in Astoria, and enjoying the rest of the world in between.

message of cross not persuasive and compelling enough in itself that God must save men against their unwillingness?"

Some of my heroes in preaching and teaching are men like John MacArthur, R.C. Sproul, John Piper, C. J. Mahaney, Mark Dever, J.I. Packer, etc. I consider them my friends and I desire to be associated with them. However, I hope there is room to uphold their legitimacy and value in the body of Christ, respect them, fellowship with them, but not be compelled to agree on all points. I hope that my Calvinist friends will not allow a new surge of Reformed theology to create a new kind of fundamentalism in which the "rightness" of Calvinism becomes the standard of Christian belief.

I am neither a committed Calvinist nor an Arminian. Frankly, I do not have a satisfactory theological label, though there is a part of me that really wants to be a Calvinist. Most of my heroes wear that label. Calvinism is associated with being biblically astute, theologically grounded, and intellectually superior. Who does not want those accolades?

Admittedly, there have been times when I have succumbed to the push of the crowd swell toward Calvinism. Sometimes it's easier to agree with the giants than to fight them. So I have worn the label, though most often it was like wearing a borrowed suit that others thought looked fine but I knew it did not quite fit well. For inquisitive and honest minds, outward conformity never quiets the internal discomfort of contradiction.

The contradiction that exists is not the ability to find enough Scripture to support the assertions of Calvinism, the contradiction (for me) is between the assertions of Calvinism and my personal understanding of God acquired through a lifetime of Bible study, preaching, counseling, and living as a disciple of Christ. The God whom I know personally causes me to look into that Chinese man's eyes and believe with passion that the God of the Bible loves him and wants that man to know Him.

Theological minds in pursuit of biblical accuracy always seek coherence. However, too often it is coherence with someone else's systematizing of Scripture, while living with internal contradiction. Yes, I have been able as a confessed Calvinist to satisfactorily exegete texts to fit the system. I can argue and offer exegetical explanations that support the points of TULIP. My Calvinist friends will applaud. My borrowed suit looks fine to them. But, I am yet uncomfortable. I still have to get on the train and look the elderly Chinese man in the eye.

Some obviously find comfort in Calvinism. I am glad for their comfort and seek not to detract from it. However, some of us have a nagging discomfort with a system that limits the love of God and intentionally shuts the door of the gospel to an "unknown many." Though we can exegetically support Calvinism, we also know that those texts can be adequately explained in a non-Calvinistic way.

So, the dilemma is this: Do I uphold the exegesis of texts that coheres to a system and allows me to be a member of the Calvin Club, while living with the internal discomfort of looking into that Chinese man's eyes and wondering if this man has no possibility of knowing the love of God; or, do I handle texts in a way that is equally honest, does not always cohere with a system, but coheres internally with my overall knowledge of God acquired over many decades as a Christian.

I am comfortable not being a Calvinist and not really knowing which system I most align with. I see the God of the Bible as creating out of all possible worlds, the world which best reflects His nature. Which of the possible world most glorifies God—one in which gracious provision is made for all who are invited to believe or a world where God predetermines who can and cannot believe and experience His love and grace? I see a world where His love and grace is expressed broadly and men are given opportunity to accept it or reject it. I see a world that displays God's sovereignty and power, but is more about His grace and His goodness. I see a world where God is more interested to include as many as will believe (Go and disciple the nations) than He is in showing His Sovereign power in limiting who can believe.

If God has not elected that Chinese man to salvation, then obviously God does not care about him. Of course, if I were a Calvinist, I could not know for whom God cares so I should care for everyone, even though it's possible that God doesn't care about him But, I'd still have to live with the contradiction of my own knowledge of God which tells me, "God so loved the world." Is this Chinese man

Calvinism on the "N" Train

part of the world? Does God's love for him include the possibility of salvation, and, equally so for the two Hispanic men sitting next to him, and the Chinese lady to my left. Even as a Calvinist, all of the exegetical gymnastics with verses such as John 3:16 never quite explained away the clarity of "God so loved the world" and "he is the propitiation for our sin, and not for ours only, but for the sins of the whole world."

I seek an understanding of Scripture that coheres with looking into the eyes of a Chinese man on the "N" train—an understanding that moves beyond "I don't know if he is elect; yet, God ordained the use of means in bringing the elect to Himself; so as a matter of obedience I should share the gospel to this man; but, if I don't witness, God will save the elect anyhow."

I seek an understanding of Scripture that coheres both with the Bible and with my own personal experience of God that tells me, "God loves and care for that Chinese man and has provided for his redemption. I should care because God cares."

Further Questions for Reflection?

- What is the determinative point of inclusion—exclusion—the cross, faith, election, etc.?
- Does the cross express primarily the love of God for many or the power of God to save a few?
- Did God call Abraham as a way of excluding all others or as a means of including more?
- When God chose the best of possible worlds, was not His character (love and omniscience) the basis of that choice? Which of the possible worlds most glorifies God—one in which gracious provision in made for all who are invited to believe or a world where God predetermines who can and cannot believe.
- Is God's greatness most seen in the display of His power or in the display of his love?
- Do sinners a have a legitimate struggle between the attraction of sin and the attraction of the grace of God?

Section Two | On Theology

- In what way does the goodness of God lead sinners to repentance?
- How does John 3:15–17 inform our understanding of election?
- How do we reconcile the compassion of God for some lost people and not for others?
- Is it God-like to weep over those who perish without Christ?
- Why would a God who has chosen to not elect some to life care about their eternal suffering?
- Why would Jesus long over Jerusalem and at the death of Lazarus for people whose destinies were already determined by his sovereign choice.
- What is chosen—the plan or the people?
- Does evangelism make a quantitative difference in the outcome of who comes to Christ?

CHAPTER NINETEEN

My *ordo salutis* on the "N" Train

I was on the "N" train again today.[1] I looked into the eyes of another Chinese man, asking myself this time, how does a sinner believe? How does one dead in trespasses and sin come to life? Does regeneration precede faith? Is it possible, as I look into the eyes of the Chinese man, he already has been or will be made alive by the Spirit because he is one sovereignly chosen by God?

Or, is it possible that his deadness means that no spiritual life is present and never can be possible, because this Chinese man may be one who is not part of God's plan? Perhaps he is not one of God's elect and all the prayer and preaching in his behalf can never have any influence in his coming to life.

Or, does his deadness simply describe the absence of spiritual life and his alienation from God without erasing the possibility that

---

1. See the footnote on p. 64. The N Train runs from Coney Island in Brooklyn to Astoria in Queens, taking the long route as an express train through Manhattan. Half the time it runs above ground including views of Brooklyn, Queens, and Manhattan as it travels across the Manhattan Bridge, and views of Astoria and Long Island City running through Queens. The route of the N Train captures the ethnic diversity of the city as it winds through Russian, Hasidic, Chinese, Italian, Hispanic, Middle Eastern, and other neighborhoods. The economic diversity of the city is also reflected in its path as it stops in a lower income area like Sunset Park, among a flurry of small businesses in Chinatown, or at the upscale stores of both 5th Avenue and Lexington Ave. If you love to eat, then you can enjoy the cuisines of the world starting with borsch in Coney Island, ending with Fried Kefalotiri cheese in Astoria, and enjoying the rest of the world in between.

he may live again? Is there a mystery, irresolvable to the human mind, regarding the knowledge and plan of God in relationship to human response?

Perhaps the answer to whether this Chinese man can believe or why I believed and my neighbor didn't is not as clear cut as "one was predestined to believe (Calvinism) or one chose on his own accord not to believe (Arminianism)."

I know someone may say, "Quit thinking so much about it and just share the gospel with him," and that is an appropriate response. Regardless of what one believes about the *ordo salutis,* sharing the gospel should be a matter of obedience and passion. And, I have observed that there is no necessary connection between one's understanding of the *ordo salutis* and his sharing of the gospel. There are both Calvinists and Arminians who are evangelistic and who are apathetic. It is more likely that biblical spirituality, more than theology, influences one's evangelism.

Nevertheless, my mind won't rest as I continue to seek a scriptural understanding of what is happening when a sinner comes to Christ.

Ordo salutis is the Latin term for "the order of salvation." One of the fruits of the Reformation is the attention given to the *ordo salutis.* The Reformed site monergism.com sets forth the following general distinction between the Calvinistic and Arminian *ordo salutis*:

> In the Reformed camp, the *ordo salutis* is 1) election, 2) predestination, 3) gospel call 4) inward call 5) regeneration, 6) conversion (faith & repentance), 7) justification, 8) sanctification, and 9) glorification. (Rom 8:29–30)
> In the Arminian camp, the *ordo salutis* is 1) outward call 2) faith/election, 3) repentance, 4) regeneration, 5) justification, 6) perseverance, 7) glorification.[2]

Though the above summaries are commonly held, if you've read enough of both Reformed and Arminian writers, you begin to realize that even among themselves, there are differences in the *ordo salutis.* Calvin himself placed faith before regeneration.

2. *The Ordo Salutis,* n.d.

My ordo salutis on the "N" Train

I am aware of the Scriptural arguments used by both systems, especially in answering the question, why and how could a spiritually dead Chinese man believe. Arminianism never really answers the question. Though Arminianism teaches the necessity of prevenient grace (a prior work of the Spirit before faith), it never resolves the question of how two people can experience prevenient grace, yet only one believes. On the other hand, Calvinism answers the question clearly. A dead man believes because he was elected, called, regenerated, then believed. Though some, like Calvin himself, would place regeneration after faith, one's faith is ultimately grounded in God's sovereign election.

On the other hand, Arminianism grounds God's election on the foreseen faith. Faith is not a consequence of election, and ultimately remains unexplained. So, in Calvinism, faith is inevitable in some, not possible for many; in Arminianism, faith is possible for all, not inevitable for any.

So where does the truth lie? Which understanding of faith is undergirded by Scripture? I confess I find here a mystery that is irresolvable to my finite mind. As I read Scripture, some appear to teach the inevitability of faith for some (Acts 13:48) and others appear to teach the possibility of faith for all (Romans 10:13). I am not satisfied that either system fully answers with complete Scriptural coherence the question of why one Chinese man believes and another does not, when both have equal access to the gospel.

Must I seek a logical and chronological order of the various aspects of salvation or is there something about the nature of salvation that any attempt to order them distorts the wonder and mystery of God's plan of redemption? After all, is not all of salvation in Christ? Can anyone have election, regeneration, justification, sanctification, glorification or saving faith without Christ? Is it not our calling to preach Christ and Him crucified? For if one has Christ, he has the whole *ordo salutis*.

Though I am aware that many are comforted by the purported *ordo salutis* in Romans 8:28-30, for me I choose the following text for an *ordo salutis* on the N train:

¹⁶ ¶ "For God so loved the world, that he gave his only Son, that whoever believes in him should not perish but have eternal life. ¹⁷ For God did not send his Son into the world to condemn the world, but in order that the world might be saved through him. ¹⁸ Whoever believes in him is not condemned, but whoever does not believe is condemned already, because he has not believed in the name of the only Son of God (John 3).

Now I realize some will read the above text differently. They may say that the world that God loved is the world of the elect. And, from other texts they may conclude that those who believe are those who have first been elected, called externally and internally, regenerated, then brought to faith. However, the simple *ordo salutis* here appears to be:

1. Unbelief
2. condemned
3. God's love
4. provision of Christ
5. available content of belief
6. belief
7. not condemned.

This *ordo salutis* seems consistent with Romans 10 and even the classic passage on election, Ephesians 1:3-14. In Ephesians 1, though verses 3-12 tells us of the benefits and blessings of God's plan of redemption (read carefully the phrases that are objects of the verbs, i.e. chosen . . . that we may be holy and blameless; in love having predestinated . . . unto the adoption of sons; having been predestined . . . unto the praise of His glory), it lays out no *ordo salutis* of how those who are *chosen in him* (not, as some imply, *chosen to be in him*) actually come to be "in him." The *ordo salutis* how one comes to be "in him" waits until verse 13:

¹³ In him you also, when you heard the word of truth, the gospel of your salvation, and believed in him, were sealed with the promised Holy Spirit,

The *ordo salutis* here is:

My ordo salutis on the "N" Train

1. heard the Word
2. believed
3. sealed.

This order also seems consistent with Romans 10:13–17 (hear, believe/call, saved).

As I look at this Chinese man in the N train, I'm still not sure "how" and "why" he may believe or may not believe, though I am confident that faith is possible and that the means God has chosen to encourage that belief is the preaching of the gospel. The tenor of Scripture is that saving faith and new life are inextricably dependent on the Word of God (Romans 10:17; 1 Peter 1:23). So, I will not just think about the Chinese man on the N train; I will somehow try to give him the Word of God.

Now you have it! You can choose between Calvinism, Arminianism, or Davisism.

SECTION THREE

On Sanctification

CHAPTER TWENTY

The Gospel and Transformation

⁷ Now if the ministry of death, carved in letters on stone, came with such glory that the Israelites could not gaze at Moses" face because of its glory, which was being brought to an end, ⁸ will not the ministry of the Spirit have even more glory? ⁹ For if there was glory in the ministry of condemnation, the ministry of righteousness must far exceed it in glory. ¹⁰ Indeed, in this case, what once had glory has come to have no glory at all, because of the glory that surpasses it. ¹¹ For if what was being brought to an end came with glory, much more will what is permanent have glory. ¹² ¶ Since we have such a hope, we are very bold,, ¹³ not like Moses, who would put a veil over his face so that the Israelites might not gaze at the outcome of what was being brought to an end. ¹⁴ But their minds were hardened. For to this day, when they read the old covenant, that same veil remains unlifted, because only through Christ is it taken away. ¹⁵ Yes, to this day whenever Moses is read a veil lies over their hearts. ¹⁶ But when one turns to the Lord, the veil is removed. ¹⁷ Now the Lord is the Spirit, and where the Spirit of the Lord is, there is freedom. ¹⁸ And we all, with unveiled face, beholding the glory of the Lord, are being transformed into the same image from one degree of glory to another. For this comes from the Lord who is the Spirit (2 Corinthians 3).

Section Three | On Sanctification

I was in a conversation recently with someone talking about a counseling situation where the young man had created an alter ego. He came from a Christian home with parents who desired the best for him so from the beginning they named him Samuel, after the prophet who obeyed God. To him Christianity was all about obeying and pleasing God and earning his favor. He knew little of grace and became weary of trying to be Samuel. So he created Saul, another personality that would rebel against God and enjoy the pleasures of sin. He would revert back and forth from Samuel to Saul, between striving to please and living for his own selfish desires. He found happiness and peace in neither personality. In themselves, neither striving to be Samuel or Saul could lead to peace. Together, eventually it led to a psychological breakdown.

Now you may say, that's pretty weird, but if you think about it, you can identify with either one of his personalities or maybe both. You live striving to please God but are wearied by it; or you live running from God and still wearied by it (or maybe you live a life of duplicity).

What the Samuel and Saul personalities have in common is that they both focus on the power of self to achieve happiness through obedience or through rebellion and the inevitable emptiness that results from both.

We are looking at text that talks about the glory of God : 1) the glory of the Old Covenant (the law) represented by the reflection on Moses" face; 2) the glory of the New Covenant represented by the person and work of Jesus Christ.

By "glory" is meant a "a reflection of who God is." It is the same God behind the glory of the law and the glory of the gospel. Both the law and the gospel reveal the holiness of God.

In the law, the holiness of God is not propitiated (i.e. to take away the wrath and displeasure)

In the gospel the holiness of God is propitiated by the blood of Christ (Romans 3:24).

In the law, the un-propitiated holiness of God induces fear (30 Aaron and all the people of Israel saw Moses, and behold, the skin of his face shone, and they were afraid to come near him.) This fear

The Gospel and Transformation

exists because when sinful beings are confronted by God's holiness they can only cry out as Isaiah the prophet did, "Woe is me!"

In fear people do one of two things: 1) they attempt to appease God by an obedience that earns his favor; 2) they run from God abandoning any hope of having his favor.

We try to manage this fear of God's glory either by running from the glory or trying to appease the glory. Either way is futile. Neither Samuel nor Saul is the model for us.

Though there is a third option: As Isaiah, we can receive cleansing from God. The law reveals to us our need of God's mercy and forgiveness. To alleviate this fear, every time Moses came from the presence of God he would put a veil over his face.

Our text, here adds a little more information about what this veil accomplished. Not only did it alleviate the fear of the law; it hid the fact that the reflection on Moses' face would have dissipated in time—it hid the fading glory—the temporary nature of the law and the true purpose of the law.

Furthermore, the people's response to the display of God's holiness revealed that another veil existed—a veil over their hearts. This veil over their hearts coupled with the veil over Moses' face brought about a distortion of the law: Because of the veil, the fear inducing holiness of God became a feint memory and the fading glory of the law was hidden so that with veiled hearts and blinded minds, the law, instead of exposing one's need of mercy, became for many the means of earning God's favor.

When the condemning and fading nature of the law are veiled and the human heart is prevented from seeing clearly the purpose of the law, the law becomes misused as a means by which to earn God's face.

Because of the veil, they could not see the outcome of the law—which is to bring us to Christ. Only in Christ do we see that the glory of the law (with its ministry of condemnation and death) has faded away and is replaced by the unfading glory of the gospel (with its ministry of righteousness and life). Christ is the end of the law to everyone who believes.

For Christ is the end of the law for righteousness to everyone who believes (Rom 10:4).

In the gospel, the propitiated holiness of God invites us to enjoy the majesty and wonder of his Holiness. In Christ, the veil is taken away from our hearts (this is the work of the Spirit in regeneration) and like Moses, with unveiled face, we come boldly into the presence of God. In contrast to Moses who hid the glory of God from the view of the people, we are bold to proclaim this unfading, life-giving and righteousness-giving glory of Christ.

Now here is the key to the relationship of the gospel and transformation in verse 18:

> As we keep beholding, we are transformed into the image of the glory of Christ.

This is the work of the Spirit who is none other than Yahweh of the OT. The same Lord who gave the law is the Lord of the gospel. How are we transformed, "while beholding" (keeping the glory of Christ, as revealed in the New Covenant, in focused view), the Spirit transforms us.

We are active in beholding the glory of Christ.

Why is this gaze upon the glory of the cross so crucial to transformation? Because the cross exposes your powerlessness and it is only in being powerless that you experience the transforming power of God.

We are passive in the transformation that takes place. This is the work of the Spirit of God. There is a similar pattern in 2 Cor 4: (being renewed while beholding)

> [16]Though our outer self is wasting away, our inner self is being renewed day by day. [17] For this light momentary affliction is preparing for us an eternal weight of glory beyond all comparison, [18] as we look not to the things that are seen but to the things that are unseen. For the things that are seen are transient, but the things that are unseen are eternal (2 Cor 4).

Where do we behold the glory of Christ? In the New Covenant in Christ, as he is revealed in Scripture, especially in the work of the

The Gospel and Transformation

gospel. The Law revealed the glory of God's fierce holiness moving the heart to fear. The gospel reveals the glory of God's propitiated holiness moving the heart to worship.

Who does the transforming? The Spirit of God.

This glory, rather than fading, increases—from glory to glory. Moses reflected an intermittent fading glory of the law; we reflect a progressively increasing glory of the gospel.

> Consider well of the office, the bloodshed, and the holy life of Christ—His office is to expiate sin, and to destroy it. His blood was shed for it: his life condemned it. Love Christ, and thou wilt hate that which caused his death. Love him, and thou will be made more like him."[1]

"Isn't it true, you know, that ultimately, we become like what we worship? If we worship money, we become materialistic. If we worship power and prestige we become cold and calloused. If we worship an idol, we become as spiritually dead and lifeless as a stone. On the other hand, if we worship Christ, we will be conformed to His image. If the veil is off and we behold the glory of the Lord that shines in the face of Jesus Christ, if He is our ever-increasing preoccupation then we are imperceptibly being transformed into His image by the Holy Spirit. This is the goal of the new covenant and this monumental verse shows us the increasing glory of sanctification that takes place by the Holy Spirit in the new covenant.

Folks, ceremonial, sacramental, sacerdotal works-righteousness systems offer us nothing. They didn't offer anything to the Corinthians and they don't offer anything to you either. All you need is Christ. All you need to do is get the veil off, look into the face of Jesus Christ, the Spirit of God begins the process of conforming you ever-increasingly into His image. That's what Christianity is. It isn't bells and whistles, it isn't candles and robes, it isn't Popes and Cardinals. Christianity is a relationship to Jesus Christ, it's a one-thing life, gazing at the glory of the Lord that shines in the face of Jesus Christ and

---

1. Fitzpatrick and Johnson, *Counsel from the Cross*, 148.

being transformed into His image. It's the relationship that matters."[2]

CONCLUSIONS

- Transformation is New Covenant centered, which is gospel-centered, which is Christ centered.
- Transformation involves our action in contemplating the glory of the Lord, primarily in the Word which we fail to read properly if we do not see the glory of Christ in the gospel
- Transformation takes place by work of the Spirit as we contemplate Christ, as revealed in the Word.
- Transformation is true freedom from trying to achieve God's favor on our own.

---

2. MacArthur, *Glory of the New Covenant*.

CHAPTER TWENTY-ONE

How Does the Gospel Transform Us?

The question of how spiritual transformation takes place is perhaps one of the more perplexing questions of Christianity. Misunderstanding the nature of spiritual transformation has disastrous consequences, such as pharisaical pride, dark despair, and even abandonment of Christianity. These sad consequences reflect either a neglect of the gospel or confusion on what the gospel actually is and accomplishes. A clear grasp of the gospel displaces pride, overcomes despair, and grounds one firmly in the love of God.

The gospel is primarily about what Christ has accomplished in his death and resurrection in behalf of sinners. Additionally, the gospel also includes His entire person and work. Essentially, the gospel is Jesus. Because the promise of the gospel is external to us in a person who lived, died, and rose again, it offers an unwavering, unchangeable hope and source of joy. The promise of the gospel is immutable, since Jesus is the same, yesterday, today, and forever.

Consequently, transformation never offers more than the gospel.

The gospel establishes and continues our acceptance before God. The gospel offers us the perfect righteousness of Jesus Christ freely imputed to us when we experience repentance from sin and faith in Christ. This imputed righteousness remains our gift from God forever. Never was there, is there, or will there be a moment when we stand accepted by God on the basis of anything other than the righteousness of Jesus Christ.

The gospel is always the unchanging source of our joy. No experience of spiritual transformation can offer more than or even compare to the joy of the gospel. The eternal, steadfast joy of the gospel overrides the fluctuating joys of our experiencing incremental transformation. The eternal, steadfast joy of the gospel remains the true joy both in the disappointments and the satisfactions of our experiencing incremental transformation.

Losing the joy of the gospel and seeking a replacement joy through any experience of incremental transformation produces the disastrous consequences of pharisaical pride, dark despair, and even abandonment of Christianity. The only stable, constantly satisfying joy is the joy of the gospel.

Transformation receives its power in the gospel. When transformation loses its dependence on the gospel, it easily becomes more about what we are doing to achieve a righteous life that reflects our spiritual disciplines than about what God is doing to produce a righteous life that reflects the power of the gospel. Certainly, the Scriptures talk both about our obedience and God's working in our life, but the primary focus of transformation is God's working through the gospel to transform our hearts and minds. William Edgar describes God's part very well:

> Only God can effect such a change... The great difference between self-generated transformation and biblical conversion is that God is the one ultimately at work to effect the change... The only way we can be transformed is by operating, in all areas of life, under the grace of God, who gives to all who believe in him unconditionally.[1]

The outward transformation of obedience is empowered by the inward transformation of a mind being filled with love and thankfulness for Christ that grows as the Spirit of God through the Word of God increasingly discloses to us the glory of Christ in the gospel.

---

1. Edgar, *Worship in All of Life*.

How Does the Gospel Transform Us?

The gospel is the fuel that sets aflame the fires of love and thankfulness which generate obedience to the will of God. Without hearts that are set aflame by the gospel, attempts at transformation remain only external and continue to produce the disastrous consequences of pharisaical pride, dark despair, and even abandonment of Christianity.

In our meditation on Scripture and listening to the Word, let us seek a prayerful dependence on the Holy Spirit that He would continue to unfold to us the glory of Christ in the gospel. Only in this way can our outward obedience be the natural fruit of gospel transformation. Transformation progressively reflects the person of the gospel.

One of the evidences of genuine conversion is that one's values, beliefs, and behavior progressively reflect the values, beliefs, and behavior presented in the Bible. Spiritual transformation reproduces gospel values in our lives. Gospel values are values that are exemplified in the life, death, and resurrection of Jesus Christ. Transformation is the process of believers being recreated in the likeness of Jesus Christ as described in the following verses:

> Do not be conformed to this world, but be transformed by the renewal of your mind, that by testing you may discern what is the will of God, what is good and acceptable and perfect (Rom 12:2).

> And we all, with unveiled face, beholding the glory of the Lord, are being transformed into the same image from one degree of glory to another. For this comes from the Lord who is the Spirit (2 Cor 3:18).

> All Scripture is breathed out by God and profitable for teaching, for reproof, for correction, and for training in righteousness, that the man of God may be competent, equipped for every good work (2 Tim 3:16–17).

Focusing on the glory of Christ in the gospel is never simply a "spiritual, naval-gazing exercise." Contentment in the joy of the gospel and dependence on the power of the gospel do not result in spiritual inertia. In the presence of ongoing sin and imperfection, gospel-centered transformation will allow for neither despair nor complacency. Despair or complacency in the life of a Christians is a warning signal that we have lost sight of the gospel of God's grace. The remedy is not to work harder but to gaze more deeply in the glory of Christ revealed in the gospel. The gospel assures us that we are loved and accepted and empowers us in our weakness. As we look to the glory of Christ in the gospel, love and thankfulness are set aflame and generate the natural flow of obedience.

Also, gospel-centered transformation will never allow for either pride or triumphalism. Whatever successes may be achieved, they are imperfect. The gospel remains the ground of our acceptance and the gospel reminds us daily that only the righteousness of Christ justifies us before a holy God—never our own righteousness.

As we remain fixed on the glory of Christ in the gospel, we experience the joy of the gospel, we experience the power of the gospel, and we experience the renewed life of the gospel.

CHAPTER TWENTY-TWO

The Congruence of Grace and Discipleship

> ¹⁰ But by the grace of God I am what I am, and his grace toward me was not in vain. On the contrary, I worked harder than any of them, though it was not I, but the grace of God that is with me (1 Cor 15:10).

I believe in gospel grace. Free undeserved grace. God's saving grace. Grace personified in Jesus. Grace that forgives and grace that transforms.

I also believe in gospel discipleship. Costly and demanding discipleship. Obedient discipleship. Life-altering and life-consuming discipleship. Discipleship that rejoices in suffering. Discipleship that says no to sin and yes to holiness. Discipleship that loves the outward facing mission of God.

I believe in the congruence of grace and discipleship. Grace that gives birth to discipleship. Discipleship that flows from grace. A grace and discipleship that are intimate friends, inseparable companions—one never found without the other. Bound together they are a missional grace and a missional discipleship—rooted in the gospel.

I see a counterfeit claim to grace. A grace without humility. A grace with an air of self-righteousness. A grace that leaves one in bondage. A grace that tolerates sins. A grace lying stagnant in mediocrity. A grace that knows no discipline and no discipleship. A religious grace, not a gospel grace.

I also see a counterfeit claim to discipleship. A discipleship without joy. A burdensome discipleship. A formulaic discipleship—compelled from without. A powerless and ineffective discipleship. A discipleship without mission. A discipleship without gospel grace.

I believe in a gospel grace that matures. Grace that fosters greater humility. Grace that grows in gratitude. Grace that loves and obeys Jesus more. Grace increasingly overwhelming us with the saving goodness of God. Grace undiminished by time. A growing grace fostering a greater discipleship.

I believe in a gospel discipleship that matures. A discipleship that invests more and sacrifices more for the gospel. A discipleship growing in love for the church. A discipleship increasingly agonizing for the lost. A discipleship that knows grace, loves grace, reflects grace.

This is the life to which Christ calls us—a life experiencing and growing in the congruence of grace and discipleship, for a life without gospel discipleship is a life without gospel grace and a life without gospel grace is incapable of producing gospel discipleship.

CHAPTER TWENTY-THREE

Growing Up into Salvation

Through faith in Christ, we are brought into union with Christ and into this wonderful experience called "salvation." 1 Peter tells us that salvation is something we possess in Christ; we anticipate more fully in Christ, and we "grow up into" in Christ. This is how he says it in 1 Peter 2:2: "Like newborn infants, long for the pure spiritual milk, that by it you may grow up into salvation."

"Growing up into salvation" is like walking through the caverns of Jeita Grotto in Lebanon. Once inside, you move from wonder to wonder, from awe to awe, from beauty to beauty. "Growing up into salvation" is a journey of moving through the unfathomable depths and breadths of God's love and grace, from wonder to wonder, from awe to awe, and from beauty to beauty. The caverns come to an end but the wonders of salvation are infinite because they reside in an infinite God.

The coming ages of eternity will never exhaust the satisfaction that comes from understanding the riches of His grace and His kindness which He has showed us in Jesus Christ.

This is why we are to long for the living and abiding Word of God through which God has chosen to reveal Himself, His purposes, and His unfathomable grace (Ephesians 2:7).

Those who have tasted the Lord's goodness long for this pure milk that both nurtures the new life in Christ and enables a growing understanding and appreciation of the grandeur of what God has accomplished and will accomplish through the work of Christ (1 Peter 2:3).

Such "growing up into salvation" requires a humble and repentant heart that looks to the gospel to be rid of those sinful hindrances that create the kind of spiritual illness in which the longing for spiritual nourishment is diminished (1 Peter 2:1).

CHAPTER TWENTY-FOUR

"My cross to bear"

Often Christians and non-believers use this phrase to describe their burden of suffering in life. Unfortunately, both of them err in understanding the context of these words given by Jesus. Listen to Jesus" words after Peter confesses that He is the Messiah:

> [21] And he strictly charged and commanded them to tell this to no one, [22] saying, "The Son of Man must suffer many things and be rejected by the elders and chief priests and scribes, and be killed, and on the third day be raised." [23] And he said to all, "If anyone would come after me, let him deny himself and take up his cross daily and follow me. [24] For whoever would save his life will lose it, but whoever loses his life for my sake will save it. [25] For what does it profit a man if he gains the whole world and loses or forfeits himself? [26] For whoever is ashamed of me and of my words, of him will the Son of Man be ashamed when he comes in his glory and the glory of the Father and of the holy angels (Luke 9).

When Jesus talks about taking up our cross, He is not talking about common human suffering, such as illness, troubled marriages, wayward children, problems at work, or shortage of money. All of these human struggles are common to both believers and non-believers. As believers living in a fallen world and in bodies that await redemption, we are not immune from the ordinary suffering of humanity. This is not our cross to bear.

However, if we understand and obey what Jesus meant when he spoke about "our cross," we will be better equipped to handle the ordinary sufferings of life common to all humanity, as well as the extraordinary sufferings of life, that come upon us because of our identification with Jesus Christ.

Bearing your cross (i.e., "take up your cross daily") means dying to self that you may live for Jesus Christ. It is the willing abandonment of a life that is centered on autonomy and a willing surrender to the Lordship of Jesus Christ. It is a willingness to lose our life as we have designed it so that we may follow Him for His glory. It is a commitment to not be ashamed of Him and His Words. Again, bearing your cross means dying to self that you may live for Jesus Christ.

The apostle Paul captured the intent of Jesus words in 2 Corinthians 5:

> [14] For the love of Christ controls us, because we have concluded this: that one has died for all, therefore all have died; [15] and he died for all, that those who live might no longer live for themselves but for him who for their sake died and was raised (2 Cor 5).

Only when we truly "bear our cross" by dying to self and living for Christ will we be able to glorify God in the ordinary suffering of life common to all humanity, and in the extraordinary sufferings of life which come upon us because of our identification with Jesus Christ.

CHAPTER TWENTY-FIVE

Clarifying the "Means of Grace"

The term "means of grace" is used by Roman Catholics and Protestants, and many evangelicals. Historically, the term comes out of the Roman Catholic Church which teaches that the sacraments (7 of them) are means by which the saving grace of God is communicated. The Reformers retained the terminology but nuanced the understanding of the sacraments (2 of them) as "the means by which saving grace is applied and confirmed."[1]

Both Roman Catholicism and Reformed Protestants institutionalize the means of grace, i.e., the sacramental means are neither available apart from institutions nor apart from the administration of ordained clergy. In many religious circles ordained men and women and religious institutions have control of the means of grace. In Catholicism, this is taken to the extreme of the church being

---

1. Unfortunately, the wording of the Westminster Shorter Catechism allows for confusing views on the sacraments as instrumental means of grace. "A sacrament is a holy ordinance instituted by Christ; wherein by sensible signs, Christ, and the benefits of the new covenant, are represented, sealed, and applied to believers" (WSC, 92). Craig Higgins of the New York Presbytery of the PCA added the following explanatory notes to the catechism. 1) "A sacrament is ordained by Christ; they are rites, involving physical elements (water, bread, wine) and actions (washing, eating, drinking), in the context of the Word of God. 2) "Note that the catechism's answer refers to "Christ and the benefits of the new covenant." In other words, not only the saving fruit of Christs work, but also Christ himself, [my underlining] is "represented, sealed, and applied to believers"" (Appendix C. Metropolitan New York Presbytery Study Guide on the Sacraments. By Craig Higgins).

the repository of God's grace which priests distribute through the sacraments. In Protestantism, denominations differ on the depth and breadth of "sacramentalism,"[2] while generally in agreement that the means of grace are available only through ordained clergy.

Recently, as I led the observance of the Lord's Table, I mentioned that I preferred to call the observance of the table an ordinance rather than a sacrament. I prefer the term "ordinance" for both baptism and the Lord's Table. They are visible signs of the gospel, instituted by Christ for His church, pointing us to the grace that God has given us in Christ. They are not means to receive the free grace of God but means by which to appreciate and value that grace.[3] Contrary to the Westminster Shorter Catechism, the "benefits of the New Covenant are "represented" but not "sealed and applied" to believers through the sacraments.[4]

The Bible does not teach that baptism and the Lord's Table are means of grace.[5] Though I appreciate much of Reformed theology, the use of the extra-biblical phrase "means of grace" creates unfortunate confusion. Sacramentalism coupled with an inordinate emphasis on the institution of the church and ordained clergy mistakenly results in one's dependence upon the church and ordained clergy to receive grace from God.

Please don't mistake what I am saying. I believe in the church, i.e. both the church universal composed of all those who confess faith in Christ alone as Savior and Lord and the local church composed of believers in a particular locality gathered for the worship

---

2. Though I understand the root of the word "sacrament," as something that is sacred, those who practice sacramentalism and sacerdotalism see both baptism and the Lord's Table and other alleged sacraments as instrumental means of grace. By "instrumental means of grace" they mean that something (i.e. grace) is given to the recipient by God through the instruments, such as baptism and the Lord's Table. Roman Catholics and Anglicans increase the number of sacraments. Protestants often refer to other acts like preaching, prayer, etc. as means of grace.

3. For clarification see J.C Ryle on *The Lord's Supper* (http://www.gracegems.org/Ryle/lords_supper.htm).

4. *Westminster Shorter Catechism.*

5. Of the 116 verses in the New Testament that speak of grace, not one of them connects grace to a sacrament or ordinance.

Clarifying the "Means of Grace"

and mission of Christ. I believe in the ordination of qualified men to the ministry of the Word. I believe in the necessity of corporate worship, Christian community, and a shared gospel mission. However, the Bible does not teach that the church is a repository and dispenser of the grace of God through the sacraments. While the New Testament teaches the priesthood of all believers, it does not teach that ordination grants anyone privileged access to grace which they can then mediate or distribute to others.

God's grace is His all-sufficient goodness that He offers us in and through the person and work of Jesus Christ (John 1:14–17). God's grace is only and always mediated through the person of Jesus Christ. When we believe God's Word and look to Christ in faith, He gives us grace directly. There are biblical means which point us to our Gracious Savior that we might look to him in faith, such as the Word, baptism, and the Lord's Table, but inherently they are not instrumental means of receiving grace. We come to God through Christ for grace. The church through its ministry of the Word and ordinances has a unique role in pointing us to the grace that is in Christ Jesus.

A faithful church will encourage you to look to Christ in faith through its preaching, its public worship, its baptisms, and its celebrations of the Lord's Table. As you look to the risen Christ in faith, you will find sufficient grace to save and sustain you. There are numerous means which can point you to the sufficiency of the grace of Christ, but that grace can only be received from God through the mediating work of our prophet, priest, and king, Jesus Christ.

SECTION FOUR

On Christian Fellowship

CHAPTER TWENTY-SIX

Christian Fellowship on the "N" Train[1]

The "N" Train runs from Coney Island in Brooklyn to Astoria in Queens, taking the long route as an express train through Manhattan. Half the time it runs above ground including views of Brooklyn, Queens, and Manhattan as it travels across the Manhattan Bridge, and views of Astoria and Long Island City running through Queens. The route of the "N" Train captures the ethnic diversity of the city as it winds through Russian, Hasidic, Chinese, Italian, Hispanic, Middle Eastern, and other neighborhoods. The economic diversity of the city is also reflected in its path as it stops in a lower income area like Sunset Park, among a flurry of small businesses in Chinatown, or at the upscale stores of both Fifth Avenue and Lexington Ave. If you love to eat, then you can enjoy the cuisines of the world starting with borsch in Coney Island, ending with Fried Kefalotyri cheese in Astoria, and enjoying the rest of the world in between.

On one hand the path of the N train reflects the wonderful God-intended and created diversity of the world in which we live; on the other hand it reflects the beautiful diversity of the body of Christ. People who ride the train often take something to read. It is not uncommon to see people reading their Bibles in Arabic, Chinese, Korean, Spanish, Greek, Russian, Romanian, Italian, etc.

---

1. I am thankful for my brother Stephen M. Davis and his contribution in the writing of this article.

99

Section Four | On Christian Fellowship

As you inquire about their interest in the Bible and discover that they are believers in Christ, you instantly experience a sense of belonging: "We are of the same family of God through faith in Jesus Christ." As you meet some of these brothers and sisters in Christ, you find people of various denominations and others without a denomination. You meet Calvinists and Arminians and those who never heard of either. You meet dispensationalists and amillennialists and others who only know that Jesus is coming. We can talk about our Christian experience, our churches, and even discover some of the doctrinal and practical differences we may have. But, on the N Train you always treasure meeting another family member and you value the unity you have in Christ.

It is this "Spirit" of family unity that we desire to retain in all our interactions with our brothers and sisters in Christ. We believe that N Train fellowship honors the Lord. It relegates systematic and ecclesial differences to a secondary place and elevates the Lord Jesus and His gospel to their central place. N Train fellowship manifests that which Jesus desired as the primary mark of his followers:

> [35]"By this all people will know that you are my disciples, if you have love for one another" (John 13).

We understand the functional difference between personal and ecclesial fellowship, i.e. that the basis upon which one church cooperates with another church differs from the basis upon which one believer fellowships with another; however, essentially all Christian fellowship is primarily personal; i.e. persons to persons. It is tragic if we allow our ecclesial and personal differences to override our family identity and destroy our fellowship with other sincere and God-honoring believers.

The question must be raised: What is the basis for genuine, universal Christian fellowship? The phrase "like faith and practice" has been an integral part of the fundamentalist identity and has become a frequent resort as a basis for enjoining separation from other brothers in Christ. Historically, "the Scriptures of the Old and New Testaments, having been given by inspiration of God, are the all-sufficient and only rule of faith and practice, and judge of

Christian Fellowship on the "N" Train

controversies."[2] This classic formula has been abbreviated to "like faith and practice" and used to describe a position based on the faith and practice of the apostles. The "faith" refers to the "faith that was once for all delivered to the saints" (Jude 3). The "practice" refers to the apostolic tradition (2 Thess.3:6) found in the early New Testament church by which faithful believers and churches can be identified. In this sense, "like faith and practice" retains its appeal as the basis for Christian fellowship.

However, in our day the phrase has been used to define a narrow basis of fellowship that goes beyond, not merely the original sense of the words, but beyond Scripture itself in truncating Christian fellowship in subjugation to peripheral issues and provincial concerns. The "faith" part has been enlarged to include interpretations which may be un-authoritatively valid but not essential to fellowship among believers. The "practice" part of this confession often evolves into a catch-all for concerns and preferences that cannot be claimed as apostolic. As a result, the unity of believers is threatened and the mission that we have received to disciple the nations endangered. Certainly, there is a danger and a tendency to minimize doctrine and to find the lowest common denominator to insure the largest fellowship possible. That is not acceptable to Bible-believers. However, neither should we seek to exclude brothers from Christian fellowship who are not excluded by the one authority we have in these matters—the Word of God.

On a practical note, one glaring example of this becomes apparent for many churches when determining support for missionaries. Missionaries are asked if they agree with the "faith and practice" of the church. That would not be problematic if churches did not then define the practice part with such restrictions (Bible versions, theological systems, dress standards, music, etc.) that only those who have mastered the art of diplomacy or evasive responses can be considered for support, or if they conform to the church's practices albeit with mental reservations. We understand that local churches have the right to require agreement in faith and practice and support those who most closely align with the church

---

2. Hodge, *Outlines of Theology,* 90.

as representatives of the church. Yet in being more restrictive than Scripture thinking that they are more right than others, many churches may lose the blessing of supporting missionaries who hold to "like faith and practice" in the true, historical sense but may not hold to some practices of the church which reflect local customs or concerns and often are of no importance in cross-cultural ministry.

In our opinion, the outworking of this mind-set in the larger community of believers is where the greater harm is done to the body of Christ. Local church practice and related issues are not unimportant and may reflect legitimate, local concerns. However local concerns are not necessarily normative and must not be elevated to a status of universals. They certainly should not be seen as reason for separation from brothers who hold to the same faith and compatible practice. We realize that "compatible practice" may cause gasps among some who find whiffs of compromise in ideas that depart from the received position. By this we contend that the faith once delivered to the saints is that body of non-negotiable truth to which we hold and to which we must return if we have in fact gone "beyond what is written" (I Cor. 4:6). While "the faith" is unchanging, our practice of applying scriptural truth to our *Sizt im Leben* changes with greater understanding of the truth. And our practice which reflects this faith must be compatible with the Word of God. Yet a brother in Christ who holds the same faith may differ in his practice, in the emphases, application, and implications of that faith.

One way in which this can be seen is the near obsession with which many American Christians hold to and defend passionately their eschatological schemas. Undeniably the coming of Christ is the purifying hope of believers (I John 3:2–3) and is an essential component of the faith. What a glorious truth! Jesus is coming again! It might come as a surprise that many Christians outside of North America, while looking for the coming of Christ, have far less interest in all the details over which much division takes place among us. The details are not without interest, the competing positions should continue to state their case, and churches and seminaries should express their preference or their conviction for a particular viewpoint.

Yet if we require "like faith and practice" in the modern sense of the phrase, i.e., agreement in areas of interpretation and application of principles—then there will be more of a tendency to seek sameness, failure to appreciate the diversity of how Scripture comes alive and takes root in every culture, and missed opportunities to be enriched spiritually and theologically in our encounters with other believers. We should not expect the faith and practice of other believers, apart of course from clear scriptural teaching and biblical commands, to exactly mirror our faith and practice. Faith must be founded on the Word of God. Practice must be compatible with the Word of God and will bear a family resemblance to the practice of other Christians but it may not be "like faith and practice" as currently and commonly expressed.

CHAPTER TWENTY-SEVEN

Gospel-Centered Tier One Fellowship

True Christian fellowship is based on Tier One commitments to the Gospel and to Biblical Moral Essentials (summarized in the Great Commandments). These Biblical Moral Essentials provide growing evidence of one's genuine experience of the Gospel. Tiers 2–4 should not constitute a basis for Christian fellowship.

The Gospel creates spiritual union with Christ and union with other believers. Biblical Moral Essentials give outward evidence of the reality of that union with Christ.

Those who lay claim to the gospel, yet deny perspicuous biblical morality, are refused both Christian fellowship.

THEOLOGY

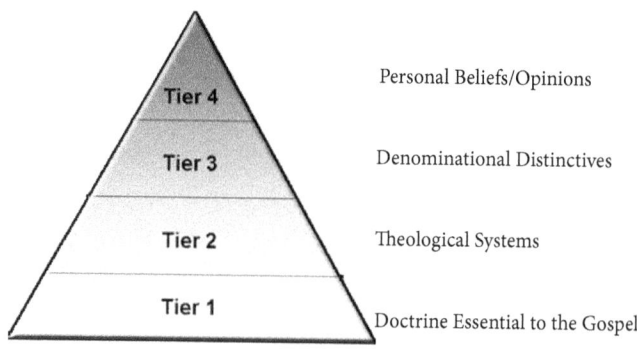

Gospel-Centered Tier One Fellowship

MORALITY

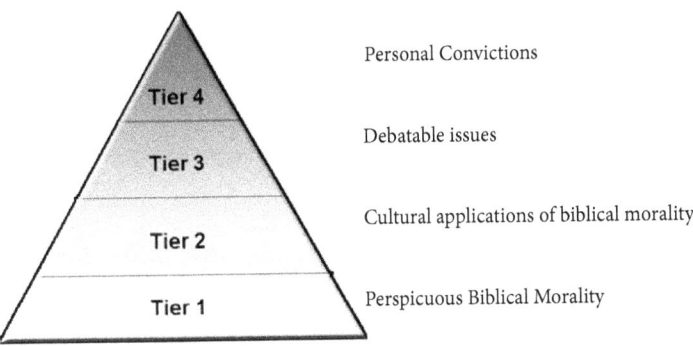

CHAPTER TWENTY-EIGHT

A Gospel-Centered Way Beyond Fundamentalism and New Evangelicalism

At Grace Church of Philly, we long for fellowship with other believers that is based upon gospel essentials. By gospel essentials, we mean those teachings of Scripture which are necessary for one to truly be called a Christian. Those gospel essentials would at least include a belief in the authority and reliability of Scripture, the Trinity, the exclusiveness and sufficiency of the redemptive work of Christ, and the depravity and inability of mankind. Also, included in those gospel essentials would be credible evidence of belief, including at least a maturing, obedient love for God and others, especially love for other believers.

Unfortunately, in the world-wide church of Jesus Christ, Christian fellowship based on gospel essentials has been difficult to achieve. This is evident in the historic divisiveness between the two movements of Fundamentalism and New Evangelicalism.

As a young Christian I was introduced to fundamentalism and thought that anyone who believed the gospel and did not agree with me on other areas of doctrine must have been a New Evangelical. I suppose that many New Evangelicals considered anyone who criticized their openness on some doctrinal matters to be a Fundamentalist. I can remember the days when John MacArthur and John Piper were considered to be New Evangelicals by Fundamentalists, though it is likely that New Evangelicals considered them both to be Fundamentalists. This common way of thinking presents a false dilemma in that it offers only two options (Fundamentalism and New Evangelicalism) and requires that you make a choice between the two.

Additionally, not only is there a false dilemma, there is an arbitrary standard of what characterizes a Fundamentalist and a New Evangelical. From Fundamentalism's vantage point, one is a New Evangelical and not a Fundamentalist, because they do not practice "biblical" separation from those who do not agree with their understanding of Scripture. From a New Evangelical's vantage point, one is a Fundamentalist and not a New Evangelical, because they practice a "non-biblical" separation from those who differ on various aspects of biblical teaching. Fundamentalists would say that New Evangelicals practice separation over nothing; New Evangelicals would say that Fundamentalist practice separation over everything.

Rolland D. McCune, a Fundamentalist, alleges that New Evangelicalism's movement away from "true Christianity" could have been prevented had they practiced ecclesiastical separation. Of course, for McCune, true Christianity includes much more than gospel essentials.

> This comes as no surprise to fundamentalists because the greatest hedge against this corruption by association (1 Cor 15:33) is the practice of ecclesiastical separation. Since the repudiation of this doctrine was probably the chief cornerstone of the new evangelicalism from its inception, the movement had a manifest destiny of deterioration in theology and ambivalence in practice from the beginning. Its antiseparatist obsession left it shorn of the God-appointed means of preserving and propagating true Christianity.[1]

Along a similar vein, Dr. Harold Ockenga, a New Evangelical who wrote the foreword to Dr. Harold Lindsell's book, *The Battle for the Bible*, published in 1976, affirms the anti-separatism of New Evangelicalism:

1. McCune, *DBSJ* 8, 85–99.

Section Four | On Christian Fellowship

> Neo-evangelicalism was born in 1948 in connection with a convocation address which I gave in the Civic Auditorium in Pasadena. While reaffirming the theological view of fundamentalism, this address repudiated its ecclesiology and its social theory. The ringing call for a repudiation of separatism and the summons to social involvement received a hearty response from many evangelicals. . . It differed from fundamentalism in its repudiation of separatism and its determination to engage itself in the theological dialogue of the day. It had a new emphasis upon the application of the gospel to the sociological, political, and economic areas of life.[2]

New Evangelicalism admittedly refused to allow its theology (including gospel essentials) to determine its ecclesiology.

Is it not possible that both Fundamentalism and New Evangelicalism have a deficient ecclesiology that diminishes the primacy of gospel essentials? McCune argues that the "greatest hedge against this corruption by association is ecclesiastic separation" to preserve what he called "true Christianity" while Ockenga argued that "while reaffirming the theological view of fundamentalism," New Evangelicalism "repudiated its ecclesiology and its social theory."

Unfortunately, Fundamentalism's understanding of "true Christianity" and basis for ecclesiastical separation was often arbitrary, unpredictable, provincial, and beyond gospel-essentials. While, New Evangelicalism was right in rejecting this aberration of separation, their lack of commitment to gospel essentials led them down a path of diluting the true nature of Christianity.

Fundamentalism and New Evangelicalism represent contrasting ecclesiologies of exclusion and inclusion. Fundamentalism has an ecclesiology that defines genuine Christianity in expanded terms including much that has no bearing on gospel essentials (such as eschatological systems, church government, etc), thereby excluding many. From a Fundamentalist perspective, agreement on all matters of faith and practice is essential and any disagreement is equivalent to disobedience and, consequently, cause for exclusion. Fundamentalism diminishes the primacy of gospel essentials by

---

2. Lindsell, *Battle for the Bible*, n.p.

A Gospel-Centered Way

elevating other biblical teaching to an equal or greater level. On the other hand, New Evangelicalism diminishes the primacy of gospel essentials by often expanding Christian fellowship to include those who reject gospel essentials.

My assessment is that if gospel essentials were rightly elevated, Fundamentalists would be more inclusive and New Evangelicals would be more exclusive. If Fundamentalism focused on the primacy of gospel essentials their appreciation of the believing church would grow to include many whom they now reject because of disagreement on non-gospel essentials. If New Evangelicalism focused on the primacy of gospel essentials their appreciation of the church would bring them to exclude those who reject those gospel essentials.

Beyond Fundamentalism and its certainty on all matters of theology and New Evangelicalism's openness to accept most everything, we desire to identify with those individuals and groups who have questioned both the arrogance of Fundamentalism and the tolerance of New Evangelicalism and who seek Christian fellowship based on gospel essentials.

> In essentials, unity
> In non-essentials, liberty
> In all things, charity

SECTION FIVE

On Pastoral Ministry

CHAPTER TWENTY-NINE

On Personality, Power, Friendship, and Integrity

Pastoring for many years has taught me a lot about myself and a lot about other Christian leaders. I had a friend early on with whom I spent a lot of time discussing ministry. He was like a mentor to me. By human standards he was a successful pastor with enormous influence. I liked being around his engaging personality and enjoying his favor. As time went on, I suspected that he often played loosely with the truth. Some would even say that he was a pathological liar. Yet, he was my friend and I excused his "imperfection" and overlooked it. As time moved on and my journey took me down a different theological and philosophical path, our friendship ended and I became the object of his innuendoes. Looking back, our friendship was not deep for if it had been, I would have confronted him along the way about his lack of integrity and he would have loved me even though I took a different path. Admittedly, as a young pastor I loved the presence of power and influence too much. Later in life, we pursued friendship again. I had experienced enough disappointment to no longer be enamored with personality and success, and he had suffered enough pain to be humbled.

One day I had a conversation with a fellow pastor who was describing the difference in the way that he and I approached ministry. He referenced my departure from the Independent Fundamentalist Baptist movement in 1988. At that point in my life, I began to realize that true Christian fellowship was undermined by the separatism and turf-protectionism of much of the IFB movement. Instead of quietly maintaining the status quo, I disclosed to my church what was going on in my life and I informed about 100 of my IFB "friends" that I would no longer practice that form of separatism. For me it was a matter of integrity. My fellow pastor contrasted my approach with his. He said, "I have chosen to not water the weeds that were sown before me and to let them die slowly." He has done that for a long time and the weeds continue to sap the life out of his soul and his ministry. I think that his method is not only a bad approach to gardening, but sets forth an example of pastoring without integrity and must eventually lead to a conflicted conscience. Looking back, I realize that the weeds I saw in my own ministry could have been yanked out more systematically and gently, but letting them die a slow death should never be the option. In most gardens, weeds grow more prolifically then flowers and plants. Pull the weeds but be gentle to the plants.

Recently, I had to go out of my way to get a seminary president's attention. After numerous emails and no response, I went to see him and asked why he did not answer my emails. His response was, "Don't take it personally. I am an equal-opportunity non-responder." Should I really believe that the president of a seminary characteristically does not respond to emails? We had breakfast together and what I thought was a movement toward reconciliation and fellowship. As it turns out, it wasn't real. He still does not follow through or answer emails. I think he really wanted to say, "We empathize with where you are theologically and philosophically, but we have supporters that might be offended by your involvement with the seminary. We must maintain the flow of money at any cost even if that means not living out who we believe God wants us to be." My desire for gospel centered fellowship with all believers causes me at times to be intentionally naïve, thinking that a common commitment to the gospel should make fellowship possible. However, I do realize that other agendas trump the gospel in Christian ministry and when that occurs, integrity can be sacrificed. Pursue peace with all men as much as it is possible. It is not always possible.

I have met a few kinds of prevaricators in ministry—those who are cowardly, always protecting their image, and those who

On Personality, Power, Friendship, and Integrity

are brazen and so intent on accomplishing their agenda that they can spin anything. I have worked with both in leadership. Sometimes there is such sophistication in lying that we must live with the suspicions until the circumstantial evidence is overwhelming. Or sometimes we choose to live with the suspicion because of friendship, personal advantage, need of a skill set, repercussions of exposing the lie, etc. Forgive me for my guilt in all the above. Most often prevaricators move on to another unsuspecting setting uncorrected and unexposed; others remain so adept at the skill of illusion that they continue to survive where they are.

Though I pursue a life of integrity, I am not without fault. My desire for approval and the idolatry of my agendas can cause me to be silent when I should speak up and can cause me to not say everything that should be said when I do speak up. At times, I may justify my approach as a matter of "wisdom" when it may just be cowardice or an idolatrous commitment to an agenda.

So, here is what I ask of my friends. Please help to keep me honest. Question me, confront me, pray for me, and encourage me to be a man of integrity. If you are suspicious, ask; if you think the facts are wrong or misrepresented, tell me; if you think there is more that I should be saying, probe me. I will do the same for you.

Is not this the call of the gospel?—to live and speak the truth in love.

CHAPTER THIRTY

Ordinary Pastors

I have in hand another invitation to a big-name conference with a big-name speaker. I could go and hang out around the coffee pot with ordinary pastors, but I am told that the important stuff comes from the important people.

My brother Steve and I have spoken from time to time on how glad we are to be part of an elder team of ordinary pastors. At Grace Church there is no single awe-inspiring individual with whom Grace Church is identified. We are not a team of great personalities. We are glad to fellowship with a movement of ordinary pastors led by ordinary men who are seeking to be faithful to the work and Word of God.

Some time ago I read Don Carson's book *Memoirs of an Ordinary Pastor: the Life and Reflections of Tom Carson* in which he told the story of the faithful work of his father laboring in small churches in Quebec. The Reformed Reader summarizes the book aptly:

> This book is not exciting. Rev. Tom Carson's life was pretty normal—though perhaps a little more difficult than average because he labored in such hard soil (the Quebec area in the "40s and beyond). He is not very quotable, and his journals aren't full of moving and inspiring writing. Rev. Carson even suffered through periods of melancholy because he didn't have a high view of himself; he sometimes questioned his abilities and calling. So if you want a book about self-motivation, conquering the world for Christ, starting a thriving ministry, or building

a multi-campus church, don't get this book. You'll be sorely disappointed.

However, if you want to see what the life of an ordinary pastor is like, this book belongs on your shelf. I'm guessing that most of our readers are in the context of a smaller church whose pastor is not known by more than a few hundred people. This book is for those pastors! And I'd encourage parishioners to read it as well, just to get an idea of what it's like to simply be a Christian pastor, father, and husband who does his best to follow the Lord in faith and obedience."[1]

I enjoy the company of ordinary pastors. Though they have written books, they have not written a book that has cast them into such prominence that they have left their church to talk about the book. They have not experienced such phenomenal church growth that they have become itinerant evangelists of church success. They do not tweet often and are rarely, if ever, re-tweeted. They have no unique and engaging story to tell that sets them apart from other ordinary pastors—at least not one that many want to listen to. They are ordinary. They seek to be 1 Timothy 3 kind of men; they are faithful in preparation and preaching; they are involved in evangelism, discipleship, shepherding, and community involvement. They are ordinary.

Because they are ordinary, they have no need of being the center of attention. They actually care about other ordinary pastors and are interested in what is going on in the lives and ministries of ordinary pastors. I have one such valued friend who over the course of our friendship has never sought to impress me with his successes but who, unintentionally, has impressed me with his faithfulness. He is an ordinary pastor who one day will hear the words, "Well done, ordinary pastor (good and faithful servant). Enter into the joy of the Lord."

May God give us more ordinary pastors and maybe even more conferences for ordinary pastors led by ordinary leaders.

---

1. Compton, *Reformed Reader*.

CHAPTER THIRTY-ONE

Extended Sabbaticals

Recently, a few high-profile Christian leaders have taken long sabbaticals from public ministry to give attention to the care of their souls. This is a luxury that most of us in and outside of ministry cannot afford but perhaps one which we all desire from time to time. However, most of us are caught up in the exigencies of daily life, family, ministry, community, etc. and depend upon the gospel to nurture our souls in the midst of the stresses and challenges of daily life.

If there is a pattern of sin in the lives of these men that disqualifies them from ministry, then I understand the extended sabbatical and would recommend that they get a job and learn to live the Christian life in the midst of the challenges of life outside of ministry.

If there is no disqualifying sin, then is this growing pattern of "extended sabbatical" a pastoral example setting forth the way for everyday Christians to deal with their sin and failures in life? Or has elitism evolved in Christianity in which a privileged few need special treatment to address their superior spiritual needs?

I do not mean to be cynical. The men whom I have in mind are men from whom I have learned much and have been encouraged in my walk with the Lord and my pursuit of faithfulness in ministry. I have read their books, listened to their sermons, and have been encouraged by them to look to the sustaining power of the gospel. I have learned from their careful exegesis and exposition, but now

Extended Sabbaticals

am a bit confused by their pastoral example. Their approach to dealing with the issues of their lives is one that cannot be followed by many. Paul's frequent admonitions to follow him as he follows Christ and his exhortations to Timothy to be an example leave me bewildered at the examples of "extended sabbaticals" which cannot be followed by most.

I am a pastor who seeks to follow the Lord faithfully, as I believe these men do. Yet, I know that I follow the Lord imperfectly. I fail my wife and often need forgiveness. I perpetually fall short of being the husband I am called to be; yet I seek grace to pursue that. I fail in my relationships with people and often need forgiveness. I perpetually fall short of the ideal of what a pastor should be, yet I seek grace to pursue it. I know of no area of my life in which I can say I have arrived. But I am on a journey of growing in grace and knowledge; a journey marked with imperfections; a journey always needing repentance and renewed faith in the gospel.

I cannot follow an example of "extended sabbatical." It is out of my reach. I need an example of transparency, humility, repentance, forgiveness, and renewed passion, but I need this example displayed in the midst of the challenges of life and ministry.

To my friends in ministry, if you have sinned in such a grievous way to disqualify you from ministry, then resign, repent, and seek restoration. I will love you and pray for you. On the other hand, if the challenges of life and ministry are revealing the imperfections of your character, then show me and those who follow you how the gospel works while facing the everyday challenges of life and ministry.

CHAPTER THIRTY-TWO

Reflections on Preaching

I write as one who loves preaching, both as a preacher and a listener, and who believes that preaching the Word is central in corporate worship. I appreciate the diversity of styles, personalities, and approaches to preaching. I have learned through the years to glean something from most preachers, though admittedly I cannot help evaluating when others preach. When I sit and listen, which probably is not often enough, I have some reasonable (at least in my mind) expectations in preaching. Here are a few of my aspirations for preaching:

1. I hope that a preacher will come to the pulpit having studied and prayed over a biblical text, having grasped its central meaning, having seized its relevance, having been moved by its message, and having seen how it points to Christ.
2. I hope that the preacher will lead me to the worship of a holy and merciful God and not distract me by either his slovenly or flamboyant manner or appearance.
3. I hope that he will not think too much about being cool or funny, or avant-garde with his theology, though he may be naturally cool or funny without trying.
4. I hope that when he stands before the people of God that he will speak as one who speaks for God. He will speak boldly (standing erect with feet square and shoulders back—not leaning on the pulpit, not crossing his legs, no hands in the pocket, not nervously shuffling back and forth), clearly (projecting his

voice beyond a conversational level, with diction that is precise, and with words that are well chosen), passionately (being personally moved by the implications of this message from God), and humbly (knowing he performs a sacred task which depends upon the Spirit's power).
5. I hope that the introduction will draw me into the message and that the body of the sermon will logically argue the main point while reflecting the biblical text, and that the conclusion will tell me what to do with what I just heard.
6. Overall, I hope for an outworking of 2 Timothy 4:1–2:

> I charge you in the presence of God and of Christ Jesus, who is to judge the living and the dead, and by his appearing and his kingdom: ² preach the word; be ready in season and out of season; reprove, rebuke, and exhort, with complete patience and teaching.

May we all be encouraged by those who have proven to be faithful in the task of preaching.

CHAPTER THIRTY-THREE

Factors that Shape Life and Ministry in the Local Church

TEACHING/PREACHING

- Exegetically informed
- Grace-oriented; gospel-centered; Christ-focused
- Theologically Coherent—Generally Reformed
- Diversity on Minor Issues—i.e. eschatology, creationism, gifts, etc.

CORPORATE WORSHIP

- God and gospel-centered
- Diverse stylistically
- Celebrative and reflective
- Blend of ancient and contemporary forms
- Participatory not performance
- Informal but ordered

Factors that Shape Life and Ministry in the Local Church

LEADERSHIP

- Modeling godliness and love
- Theologically informed
- A passion for God, for the church, and for the lost
- Sacrificial and serving
- Humble and deferring

EVANGELISM

- Every day by everyone
- Relational and Strategic
- Relevant and Considerate
- Prayerful and patient
- A dance not a war
- A process not an event

SMALL GROUP RELATIONSHIPS

- Accepting and affirming
- Committed to Community
- Transparent and forgiving
- Growing in grace and knowledge

MINISTRIES

- Committed to Serve Others
- Mercy-oriented

Section Five | On Pastoral Ministry

- Teamwork
- Mission-oriented
- Excellence and effectiveness
- Accountable to the Leadership
- FAT people (Faithful, Available, Teachable)
- Involving others

STEWARDSHIP

- Care for physical property
- Fiscally responsible
- Generous
- Grace-giving
- Pursuing Quality and excellence

LIFESTYLES

- Biblically informed
- Empowered by Grace
- Ruled by love
- Pursuing Holiness
- Non-judgmental
- Deferring to others

CHAPTER THIRTY-FOUR

Why I Continue to Evangelize Other Christians

"Christian" is a broad term that includes millions who have various understandings of the person and work of Jesus Christ, who identify with a myriad of Christian institutions, and who do many good works in Jesus name. Yet, despite vast theological differences that exist among Christians, there is a persistent call for unity. The rise of Islam throughout the world, the deterioration of Christian values in the west, and the design to remove all vestiges of Christianity from the public sphere contribute to the growing rapprochement among those who call themselves Christians.

If Christianity is divided, so it is argued, then God's love is misrepresented to the world and, if divided, it will be unable to withstand the social and political attacks it suffers in the 21st century. Consequently, there is a rising cry for Christians to not proselytize from other Christian groups. This move to "Christian unity" is represented by both ECT (Evangelicals and Catholics Together) and the WCC (World Council of Churches) who call for an end to proselytizing, as well as others. Listen to the voice of those involved with ECT:

> Three observations are in order in connection with proselytizing. First, as much as we might believe one community is more fully in accord with the Gospel than another, we as Evangelicals and Catholics affirm that opportunity and means for growth in Christian discipleship are

Section Five | On Pastoral Ministry

> available in our several communities. Second, the decision of the committed Christian with respect to his communal allegiance and participation must be assiduously respected. Third, in view of the large number of non-Christians in the world and the enormous challenge of our common evangelistic task, it is neither theologically legitimate nor a prudent use of resources for one Christian community to proselytize among active adherents of another Christian community [underline is mine].[1]

Similarly, the WCC says:

> Despite all efforts to combat it, the problem of proselytism is still with us, causing painful tensions in church relationships and undermining the credibility of the Church's witness to God's universal love. Ultimately, proselytism is a sign of the real scandal which is division. [underline is mine] By placing the issue of proselytism in the context of church unity and of common witness we suggest a perspective which makes it possible to approach the problem within an adequate theological framework.[2]

On the one hand, I agree that Christian churches should not proselytize from other Christian churches when churches agree on the essential promise of the gospel, *i.e.* through faith alone in the finished work of Christ on the cross and His resurrection from the dead, sinners are brought into immediate and complete reconciliation with and justification before God; thereby rejecting any notion of saving grace mediated through the church or through the addition of any human work. The gospel asserts the sufficiency and completeness of the work of Christ in redemption removing any suggestion that our acceptance before a holy God is an unfinished process.

Wherever the gospel is blurred, diluted, or rejected I will continue to evangelize. I will evangelize "Christians" who depend upon the church and its sacraments to gradually infuse God's saving grace into them; I will evangelize those whose clearest understanding of

1. *Evangelicals and Catholics Together.*
2. *Towards Common Witness.*

being a Christian is "I was baptized" or "I go to Church" or "I receive Jesus every week in communion" or "I try to live by the ten commandments or the golden rule."

CHAPTER THIRTY-FIVE

Obsession with Urban Church Planting

One night I received a tweet and a re-tweet from a conference in Alabama on church planting. The tweet was from one of the sessions there on church planting and unfortunately tweets have no context in which to interpret them. So, I will discuss the tweet as it is. The tweet was about the speaker's bewilderment over what he called "the urban obsession with church planting when half of the world's population lives in rural areas."

In response I tweeted: "Urban obsession counteracts a history of rural obsession that neglected half of the world's peoples."

My point and the point of any urban church planter is not that we should disregard rural and suburban church planting but that in recent history urban church planting has been a neglected focus of the church and a renewed emphasis on cities is needed.

No one should debate the need of people both in rural and urban areas to hear the gospel of God's saving grace. We thank God for every church planter who seeks to invest his life in reaching the lost through church planting wherever that may be.

We make the appeal for urban church planting and are "obsessed" with it only because it makes more sense to us, as I would hope that those in rural church planting have reasons that make sense to them.

Here are some reasons why urban church planting makes sense as a legitimate obsession.

Obsession with Urban Church Planting

1. Urban church planting makes sense because this appears to be the priority of the first church planting movement under Paul.[1]
2. Urban church planting makes sense because the "cultural and intellectual flow" is more often from cities outward.
3. Urban church planting makes sense because there has been such an exodus of Christians from the cities.
4. Urban church planting makes sense because established churches in the city are dying or have died.
5. Urban church planting makes sense because immigrants from the nations of the world are more often attracted to cities, making "disciple the nations" more accessible.
6. Urban church planting makes sense because 70% of church planting already takes place outside of cities (churchplanting.com).
7. Urban church planting makes sense because it provides a more diverse[2] context to display the reconciling power of the gospel.
8. Urban church planting makes sense because cities contain more of the neglected and disenfranchised people of the world.[3]
9. Urban church planting makes sense because disillusioned, "Christianized" and "suburbanized," young people are seeking an idolatrous refuge in cities.
10. Urban church planting makes sense because the sheer density and proximity of people makes more possible and pervasive the opportunity to practice the commands to "love your neighbor" and "let your light shine among men."
11. Urban church planting makes sense because some of us simply love density and diversity and the absence of homogeneity.

Those of us doing urban church planting confess our obsession. We believe it is a good and God-honoring investment of lives and that it is so good that we want to persuade other to prayerfully consider the city.

---

1. This is not to say we hold a "biblical trump card." We recognize that a pattern is not necessarily a prescription.
2. This diversity is economic, racial and ethnic, educational, etc.
3. I am aware that the growing urbanization of the rich is producing a growing suburbanization of the poor.

Section Five | On Pastoral Ministry

For those of you doing rural and suburban church planting, I hope and pray that you will be so convinced of the value of what you are doing that you will have the kind of holy obsession that attracts others to join you in your worthwhile endeavor for the gospel.

CHAPTER THIRTY-SIX

The True Value of My Life's Work

The apparent success of the wicked and the seeming triumph of evil may lead us to ask questions about God and about the investment of our lives. We may not verbalize these questions; nevertheless, there are real questions that arise. Have you ever asked these questions? Does it pay to do the right thing? Does living for Christ really matter? Does it really matter what I invest my life in as long as I'm happy doing it?

In Habakkuk 2:12–13 the prophet, as he addresses ancient Babylon, indirectly speaks to these questions. We could summarize those questions in this way: *What determines the true value of my life's work?* These verses suggest a couple of things to keep in mind when evaluating the true value of one's life's work.

First of all, present success or failure does not measure the true value of one's life work. The ancient Babylonians built a successful empire. Through their ruthlessness and greed they conquered the nations around them. The splendor of their kingdom was world-renowned. They even boasted one of the alleged Seven Wonders of the World—the Hanging Gardens of Nebuchadnezzar. Babylon did what was necessary in order to succeed. There was no life so precious that it couldn't be sacrificed on the altar of success and no law so righteous that it couldn't be broken, if breaking that law brought about success. Babylon succeeded! But, did she really? God has only one word for those who achieve success in this manner—WOE!

God has decreed judgment on those who simply measure the value of a life's work by its apparent success.

The death of Jesus Christ on the cross may be viewed as a colossal failure from a human perspective. However, from God's perspective, that failure is the investment of a life that brings the greatest and the longest return, i.e., eternal life.

A second thing to keep in mind when evaluating the true worth of one's life work is this: Only God determines the value of one's work and energy. Verse 13 says, *Has not the LORD Almighty determined that the people's labor is only fuel for the fire, that the nations exhaust themselves for nothing?*

We may work productively and be exhausted from all the energy we've expended! For what purpose—to what end? At the end of the day, or the week, or the month or year, or at the end of your life, how do you determine the true worth of your life's work?

For Babylon the determination was clear. All that which their labor produced served only to fuel the fire. All of their energy, and time, and resources were finally measured as nothing. Historically, the Hanging Gardens were so completely destroyed that some even question whether they ever existed.

Would you consciously invest your life in what you knew to be a worthless enterprise? I doubt it! Suppose I said this to you: "I need you to help me with something. Would you please go to the supermarket and stand in the aisle for 20 minutes? Wouldn't your first question be "WHY?" Don't you find it unusual that you should ask "why" about a 20-minute investment of your life, when you may not have done the same with the entire scope of your life? Someone has aptly said, "Only one life will soon be past; only what's done for Christ will last." At the end, what will your Creator-Redeemer say about the value of your life's work?

CHAPTER THIRTY-SEVEN

What I would look for in a Seminary!

- It is decisively gospel-centered, where the exaltation of the person, work, and words of Jesus Christ holds priority over everything and is the sieve through which everything else is tested.[1]
- If in a church setting, it is one where the above principle is modeled.
- If in a church setting, it is one which is missional and shows a commitment to urban church planting and world-wide church planting, especially in the allocation of its resources.
- It practices a gospel-centered collegiality and sharing of resources with other evangelical seminaries, especially those in the same locality.
- It has professors who are discerning and generous enough to glean from and teach from the best of evangelical theologies which contribute to being gospel-centered.[2]
- It has professors who are gospel-centered enough to respect a diversity of evangelical views in the classroom.

---

1. This gospel-centeredness would be reflected in its hermeneutic, its theology and exegesis, its practical theology, its fellowship, etc.
2. Teaching their own distinctives and systems, yet with a generosity to other evangelical systems.

- It has professors who are practitioners with a heart for urban church planting and for church planting world-wide and who spend part of their tenure working in urban churches and all of their tenure in pastoral work.
- It requires first year students to do at least a one-year internship in an urban gospel-centered church[3] that is either a church plant or a church planting church.
- It has a student body that reflects a theological, ethnic, and economic diversity.
- It has urban church planting and world missions as part of its core curriculum.[4]
- It has a curriculum that never loses sight of the big story of the Bible of what God accomplishes for humankind and the cosmos through the person, work, and words of Jesus Christ.
- It garners the support of gospel-centered churches regardless of their denominational affiliation or differences in second-tier theological commitments or their differences on second-tier moral issues.[5]

---

3. Regardless of denominational affiliation

4. Regardless of where one ends up in ministry, cities are the cultural centers in the world and World Missions is a non-negotiable; therefore, everyone in ministry should be well-informed of both.

5. First-tier theological commitments are those Scriptural beliefs which are essential to the gospel, i.e. the essence of what it means to be a Christian in all times and in all places. First-tier moral issues are those unequivocal Scriptural precepts that are held in consensus by Christians in all times and in all places.

SECTION SIX

On Ecclesiology

CHAPTER THIRTY-EIGHT

New Covenant Israel in the City

The promise to Abraham that his descendants would multiply and become a blessing to the nations is fulfilled in the person and work of Jesus Christ. That ancient promise was the means through which God intended to remedy the rebellion of the human race. God chose the nation of Israel to be the people through whom he would regather the nations and restore His kingdom in the world. The repeated failure of Israel to live up to her calling created a longing for the one true Israelite who would fulfill that calling. Jesus is the quintessential Israelite.

The church is established as the New Covenant Israel with the foundation of twelve Jewish apostles and the cornerstone of the Jewish Messiah. The church does not replace Israel but rather is New Covenant Israel, i.e. Israel as God intended her to be. Israel is reconstituted at Pentecost, as the prophecy of Joel is fulfilled with the Spirit coming upon 3000 Jewish men and the apostles and others and with Peter announcing the Messiah to the *men of Israel* and to the *house of Israel* (Acts 2:22 and 2:36).

New Covenant Israel, the church, is born at Pentecost. The church as the body of Christ, the quintessential Israelite, is no less Israel than its head. Because of her union with Christ, the quintessential Israelite, the church is Israel as God intended her to be. She is a spiritual building with a Jewish foundation and a Jewish cornerstone, gathering in both Jews and the nations as God intended for Israel.

As the story of the Acts of the Apostles unfolds, this New Covenant Israel accepts immediately her calling to gather in the nations of the world, taking the gospel from Jerusalem to the ends of the earth.

As the people of the Messiah, we have the calling of ancient Israel, to gather the nations in worship of the Creator redeemer God. By His grace we have been engrafted into the life-giving vine, Jesus Christ and called to invite others to share this life. We desire to share this grace with both Jews and the nations of the world. Providentially, at this time in history, God has made the carrying out of our task more accessible by bringing the nations of the world to cities like Philadelphia. Perhaps you have been sensing a deeper longing to fulfill your calling of seeing the blessing of Jesus the Messiah come to the nations of the world. Maybe right there in your community you can share the good news with those from many nations or, if you live in a homogeneous community, God may be calling you to the city to experience how the gospel creates a new community of diverse people.

CHAPTER THIRTY-NINE

Why we use the Apostles' Creed at Grace Church of Philly

From time to time I hear concerns from well-meaning people questioning our use of the Apostles' Creed. Most often it has to do not so much with the content, but with their personal history of having recited it in the Roman Catholic Church or a liberal denominational church. Part of their conversion story is that in understanding the gospel of salvation by faith alone in Jesus Christ, they left a religious system that had corrupted and confused the gospel. We rejoice with them in their conversion and their choice to leave a faulty religious system.

However, in our use of the Apostles' Creed and other ancient creeds we are reclaiming from corrupt religious systems what belongs to historic Christianity. The content of the creed is thoroughly biblical and generally accepted by evangelicals around the world. Though there are some nuances of how one understands "he descended into hell," most would agree there is a biblical basis for the idea. We choose in our recitation to omit it. Others are offended with the phrase "holy catholic church" because they mistakenly associate "catholic" with Roman Catholic. Actually, catholic is a good word that highlights the universal, worldwide expression of the church of Jesus Christ. We replace "catholic" with Christian to accommodate some of those sensibilities and misunderstandings.

The creed simply sets forth an ancient, historic representation of the Christian faith. It does not set forth how one becomes a

Christian. Yes, it is possible to believe and recite the creed and not be a Christian, just as it is possible to recite the Lord's Prayer or pray a "sinner's prayer" and not be a Christian. Nevertheless, the creed is helpful as a catechetical tool for believers but only secondarily as an apologetic tool for unbelievers. We understand that both believers and unbelievers need more than the creed.

Admittedly, though we recite the creed regularly at Grace Church of Philly, we are not totally satisfied with the creed, i.e., not because of what it says but what it does not say. Had I been on the "creed editorial committee," I would have made the atoning work of Christ clear. For some reason I was not invited to that committee. Here at Grace Church of Philly, we are committed to being gospel-centered. The gospel is the good news that Jesus the Redeemer-King has come. At the heart of the good news is "Christ died for our sins." Since there is no substitutionary atonement in the creed, there is no preaching of the gospel in the creed. That is why I say that the creed is primarily a catechetical tool for believers not an apologetic tool for evangelism. It is both a personal and corporate confession and a teaching tool for those who already understand and believe the gospel.

In contexts where the gospel has been eviscerated, the Apostles' Creed is nothing but vain repetition, as is the recitation of the Lord's Prayer and the singing of "Holy, Holy, Holy" by many Roman Catholics, many Orthodox churches, and all theological liberals. But, in contexts where the saving gospel of Jesus Christ is central, the creed reaffirms elements of the historic Christian faith. When recited by those whose hearts are being transformed by the gospel, the Apostles' Creed becomes a hearty, personal and corporate confession of Christian belief, not vain repetition.

The confession which begins with, "I believe in God the Father, Almighty, Maker of heaven and earth . . .," is rooted in what we have already confessed and continue to confess, "that Christ died for our sins according to the Scriptures, and that he was buried, and that he rose again the third day according to the Scriptures."

CHAPTER FORTY

A Community of Witness

1 Peter 2:9-12 ⁹ But you are a chosen people, a royal priesthood, a holy nation, a people belonging to God, that you may declare the praises of him who called you out of darkness into his wonderful light. ¹⁰ Once you were not a people, but now you are the people of God; once you had not received mercy, but now you have received mercy. ¹¹ Dear friends, I urge you, as aliens and strangers in the world, to abstain from sinful desires, which war against your soul. ¹² Live such good lives among the pagans that, though they accuse you of doing wrong, they may see your good deeds and glorify God on the day he visits us.

1 Peter 2:1-12 offers insight to the kind of new community that God forms as believers live as exiles and strangers in this world. Verses 1-3 describe a community of the word; verses 4-8 a community of worship; and verses 9-12 a community of witness.

There are two statements in 2:9-12 that remind us of the twofold practice of a witnessing community:

- ... that you may declare the praises of Him who called you out of darkness into his wonderful light.

Section Six | On Ecclesiology

- ... that they may see your good deeds and glorify God on the day he visits us.

Our witness must be the harmony of lip and life, of word and of action.

Good deeds without a verbal declaration of the gospel leave people interested but ignorant of the truth. Great talking about the gospel without a credible life leaves people with information but confusion because of the hypocrisy. Peter encourages us to become a credible witnessing community by first reminding us of whom we are in Christ (vv. 9–10).

In Christ, God creates a new humanity, a chosen race identified by the gospel. This new people have a royal standing in which everyone has priestly access to God. Their nationhood is marked out not by geography but holiness. They are a people belonging to God.

Knowing that God in His mercy has granted us this status of being His people, we are compelled by gratitude to proclaim the excellence of the One who called us out of darkness into the light.

However, that proclamation must be more than words. It proceeds from a life which is experiencing inner grace and is expressing outward grace. Because we are His newly created people, we seek by His grace to have a godly interior life in which our passions are governed by the Lordship of Christ instead of our former self-centered and idolatrous pursuit (v.11).

As our inner passions are governed by the Lordship of Christ, we then can enjoy the freedom to pursue exemplary living among those who do not confess Jesus as Lord (v.12).

Consequently, as a result of a consistent witness of word and deed, those who resist will experience His grace and one day will glorify Him.

May we all experience God's grace in such a way that our lives shine brightly for His glory and our lips speak readily of His grace.

SECTION SEVEN

On Ecclesiology

CHAPTER FORTY-ONE

"catholicity"—Institutional, Incarnational, or Impossible

"catholicity" (small "c") is used in at least two ways among non-Roman Catholics: 1) the spiritual unity of the universal church, i.e., the unity of all believers in the gospel of Jesus Christ; 2) the continuity of a particular church group with the apostolic church. Wikipedia offers this explanation of the second definition of catholicity:

> The Eastern Orthodox, Oriental Orthodox, Anglicans, Lutherans and some Methodists believe that their churches are catholic in the sense that they are in continuity with the original universal church founded by the Apostles. The Roman Catholic, Eastern Orthodox, and Oriental Orthodox churches all believe that their church is the only original and universal church. In "Catholic Christendom" (including the Anglican Communion), bishops are considered the highest order of ministers within the Christian religion, as shepherds of unity in communion with the whole church and one another (http://en.wikipedia.org/wiki/Catholicity).

Wikipedia could add to the list of those who lay claim to apostolic continuity certain groups of Baptists, such as Landmark Baptists. Having been at one point in my ministry an adherent of the "Trail of Blood" mentality, I understand the desire of a particular group to be the "one true expression of the apostolic church."

145

Section Seven | On Ecclesiology

Unfortunately, this desire is most often rooted in human pride, rewritten history, and sparse exegesis of the Scriptures. In seeking to establish and maintain the "catholicity" of any particular group, true catholicity, i.e. the spiritual unity of the universal church, is undermined.

True catholicity is brought about by work of the Holy Spirit who brings all believers into union with Christ and therefore with each other. True "catholicity" is determined by the gospel and those essentials of Christianity that undergird the gospel, such as expressed in the Apostles' Creed.

The external experience of true catholicity must be incarnational not institutional. By incarnational I mean that believers must embody gospel-centered values that bring the reality of Spirit-created catholicity into Christian practice. Where the gospel and gospel values are central in the lives of believers, then despite denominational and institutional differences, there arises a commitment to practice the reality of unity that already exists, i.e. the spiritual unity of all believers. When the gospel is central and gospel-centered values are embodied, then the external expression of catholicity becomes possible and is pursued wherever and whenever believers cross paths. Gospel-centered values make catholicity a practical reality both locally, cross-denominationally, and globally.

When institutions and denominations elevate their doctrinal distinctives so that these distinctives become the expression of "true, apostolic Christianity," then the goal of genuine gospel-centered catholicity is undermined by the pursuit of an alien, denominationally-defined catholicity. Denominationally or institutionally defined catholicity makes genuine catholicity impossible. The unity to which the Bible calls us is possible only when temporal denominations, institutions, and particular churches are subordinated to the Spirit-created body of Christ brought about through union with Christ.

On the other hand, genuine catholicity is not against denominations. There are many benefits to belonging to a larger group that has a worldwide institutional presence and ministry. Nor is genuine catholicity in conflict with one's commitment to a local church that has an institutional presence and ministry in a particular locality.

"catholicity"—Institutional, Incarnational, or Impossible

There are denominations and local churches that maintain a doctrinal distinctiveness while expressing a gospel-centered catholicity to all believers. In these types of denominations and churches, there is no claim to be the sole representative of apostolic Christianity. Rather there is an adamant gospel-centeredness, a humility that accompanies the pursuit of doctrinal clarity, and a desire for incarnational gospel-centered unity in the universal church.

I confess that early on in my ministry I had an over-exalted view of the local church (especially the one I was leading) and a greatly diminished view of the church universal. Back then I had no concept of "catholicity." Probably, catholicity was equated with unbelieving ecumenism. Today I realize the goodness of a believing ecumenism and that believing ecumenism is essentially, catholicity. I still have an exalted view of the local church but an even a grander view of the church universal. I pray that God will enable Grace Church of Philly to be a local church that contributes to true catholicity

While we presently struggle with our own sinfulness that hinders catholicity, we seek God's grace to live peaceably with all men, especially those of the household of faith and we long for the ultimate external expression of catholicity at the resurrection day when all believers gather before the throne of Jesus and with one voice worship Him.

> Revelation 5:8–10 [8] And when he had taken the scroll, the four living creatures and the twenty-four elders fell down before the Lamb, each holding a harp, and golden bowls full of incense, which are the prayers of the saints. [9] And they sang a new song, saying, "Worthy are you to take the scroll and to open its seals, for you were slain, and by your blood you ransomed people for God from every tribe and language and people and nation, [10] and you have made them a kingdom and priests to our God, and they shall reign on the earth."

CHAPTER FORTY-TWO

The Weekly Celebration of the Lord's Table

At Grace Church of Philly our weekly celebration of the Lord's Table visibly and tangibly expresses the centrality of the gospel in the life of the church. At the Table, God places before His people the best nourishment that He can offer—the atoning work of His Son, as represented in the bread and wine. At the Table, we receive that nourishment as we look in faith to Jesus Christ as represented in these elements. As we physically taste and experience the bread and wine in eating and drinking, we also spiritually experience His nourishment in our coming to and believing in the One, who died for sinners and rose again.

The weekly observance of the Lord's Table affirms our ongoing need of the gospel, i.e. the basis of our relationship with God is always the death of His Son. Our progress in sanctification is deficient and can never commend us to God on our own merits. Christians always need the gospel. This is what we declare in our weekly observance of the Lord's Table.

In the order of our worship (liturgy) we observe the Lord's Table after the message from God's Word. Our participation at the Table embodies our response to God's Word. In the hearing of God's Word we have seen the greatness of God and are called to obedience, to confession of sin, and to the sufficiency of the redeeming work of Christ. We are called to worship Him. So, we come to Christ, as represented in the bread and wine, because we

The Weekly Celebration of the Lord's Table

need either cleansing from sin or power to obey (or both) and these can only be found in the gospel. As we come in faith and eat and drink, we worship Jesus Christ.

At the Lord's Table we gather as one body eating of the one bread and wine. Whatever human distinctions exist in the church, they are meaningless at the Table. We all come as sinners in need of Jesus—rich and poor, black and white and Asian, men and women, young and old. We rise from our seats together and come together to receive the bread and wine. We eat and drink together. We are one in our need and one in our looking to Christ to meet that need. Weekly as we celebrate the Table, we declare our unity in the gospel of Christ.

Our weekly observance of the Lord's Table is neither legalistic nor faddish. We do not insist that all churches must follow our pattern. In our commitment to gospel-centered worship and ministry, this weekly celebration strengthens us. We worship Christ; we are nourished by Christ; we are united in the gospel.

Come join us! There's a place at the Table for you.

CHAPTER FORTY-THREE
A Qualified Egalitarianism

1 Peter 3:1 "Likewise, wives, be subject to your own husbands..."

In the Hellenistic world of the 1st Century, women generally had a submissive role in society. There was little or no sense of egalitarianism, i.e., the full equality of men and women in ancient cultures. A woman's role, not only in relationship to her husband but to men in general, was seen as having lesser value. Paul Achtemeier puts it this way:

> Dominant among the elite was the notion that the woman was by nature inferior to the man. Because she lacked the capacity for reason that the male had, she was ruled rather by her emotions, and was as a result given to poor judgment, immorality, intemperance, wickedness, avarice, she was untrustworthy, contentious, and as a result it was her place to obey.[1]

In footnoting that paragraph, Achtemeier references Plutarch, Seneca, Petronius, Plato, Josephus, Tacitus and others. There were always women in society who resisted this role of blanket subservience, but for the most part this was the plight of women in the First Century world.

---

1. Achtemeier, *First Peter*, 206.

A Qualified Egalitarianism

Peter speaks to wives who have become believers in the midst of this world. Along with other believers, these women are called aliens of the dispersion—people who belong to the kingdom of Jesus yet are living in the kingdom of Caesar. These wives are among those who are chosen of God, with a living hope, and an unearthly joy. They are called to be holy, to live in reverence, and to love the church. They belong to a community of the word, a community of worship, and a community of witness.

How then does the gospel transform the way they live in relationship to their husbands and to other men? What Peter calls believing wives to do is not maintain the status quo but to practice a new willing submission to their own husbands that seeks to glorify God. In emphasizing this submission "to your own husbands," he also implies a new understanding for all women within societies that denigrate the value of women.

A Christian wife's view of submission to her husband is transformed by no longer viewing it as an imposition of a society that devalues women but rather as the will of God for her life. Peter upholds the headship of the husband (whether he is a believer or not). Though he does not argue for this headship, as Paul does, based on creation order, we can assume that Peter held the same view. That is, that submission is not something that is inherently evil; that it existed before the fall, that it is modeled within the Trinity's redemptive roles, and that ultimately the headship of a husband reflects the headship of Christ over His church. A Christian wife's submission is now her willing choice to glorify God.

Peter furthers implies how the gospel transforms a Christian woman in the midst of society by emphasizing that her role of submission is in regard to her own husband. There is no indication in Peter that a woman is submissive to men in general except in that all believers are to be marked by a spirit of submission. Though Peter (1 Pet 5:1–4) would uphold with other New Testament writers that the household of faith (the church) has male leadership as does the home, his call here for a woman to submit herself to her own husband leads us to believe that Peter accepts not only the male leadership of creation order but the equivalent value and responsibility of male and female in creation order.

In God's creation order (Gen 1:26–28), male headship was never intended to diminish the fact that women are made in the image of God and that women equally with men are given the mandate to take dominion of the world. This implies the full development of their giftedness and resources in all of life, though in a marriage relationship, there would be deference to a husband's leadership.

However, we also recognize that the entrance of sin into the world disturbs the good order of creation and that a husband's headship often becomes abusive and oppressive and a wife may resist and contest her role in submission. We see also how sinful thinking allows society to take a leap from submission in the home to thinking this means women are of lesser value or importance in the home to then thinking that submission of women applies to all areas of life.

The gospel says to Christian wives, "your willing submission to your husband is God's will for your life." The gospel also says, "You were made in the image of God to employ alongside of men all of your giftedness in all of life. The gospel seeks to restore in you the dignity and dominion for which God created you."

CHAPTER FORTY-FOUR
Baptism and Church Membership

The constitution of GCP states the following as one of the requirements for membership at Grace Church:

> Article 4.B. 3: Christian baptism administered by a church with an evangelical commitment to the gospel is a prerequisite for membership at GCP. We administer only believer's baptism by immersion.[1]

In light of our commitment to believer's baptism by immersion several questions arise regarding baptism itself and church membership:

REGARDING BAPTISM

Why do we baptize only believers?

We believe that the clear command of Scripture is to baptize those who confess Christ as Savior and Lord (Rom 10:9–10; Matt 28:19–20) and that this "believer's baptism" is also the most apparent pattern in the New Testament (Acts 2:42). We recognize that many of our brethren who share a similar commitment to the gospel of Jesus Christ disagree with us in that they baptize the children of believing parents. They do so, based on a commitment to the covenantal unity of the Bible and what they see as a parallel to circumcision of infants in the Old Testament and what they believe

---

1. *Constitution of Grace Church of Philly.*

is "household baptism" in certain New Testament passages (Acts 16:31–32). Though we agree on many aspects of the covenantal unity of the Bible, we recognize that the New Covenant introduces some discontinuity and with it a new sign of the New Covenant.

The Old Covenant sign was largely ethnic, placed upon children unwittingly, was associated with a revocable covenant, and was gender specific, i.e. males only.

The New Covenant sign crosses all ethnic barriers, is willingly received by believers, is associated with an irrevocable covenant, and recognizes the spiritual equality of men and women.

We practice" household baptism" in those cases where all in the household believe together and rejoice together, as is the indication of the New Testament passages where it occurs.

Clearly, if your parents had you baptized because they believed that water could wash away your sins, your parents, though sincere, did not understand the gospel. Also, if your parents had you baptized believing it to be a sign of a covenantal promise of eventual salvation, though they were sincere and well-meaning in their commitment to Scripture, we believe they misunderstood aspects of the Old Covenant and New Covenant. We believe it should be your personal joy to publicly declare your commitment to be a disciple of Jesus Christ by receiving believer's baptism, the sign of the New Covenant. If at some point you become persuaded by Scripture regarding believer's baptism, we would share in your joy by administering this ordinance to you.

Why do we baptize by immersion?

The sequence of baptism to faith is a greater theological issue than the amount of water (mode) used in baptism. Nevertheless, we practice baptism by immersion for a number of reasons.

- Though the Greek word for baptism is used in instances where immersion is not demanded, the normal usage of the word is to submerge, dip, immerse.

- Though pouring or sprinkling water offers a picture of anointing or cleansing, immersion offers a clearer picture of the Spirit's work in the gospel bringing us into union with the death and resurrection of Jesus Christ (Rom 6:1–4). This is not a divisive issue with us but we choose this mode as that which we believe best represents the teaching of the New Testament.[2]

What is the relationship of baptism to church membership?

We understand that the biblical pattern is for one's public confession of discipleship in baptism to precede the privilege and responsibility of church membership (Acts 2:41–42).

REGARDING CHURCH MEMBERSHIP

What are the benefits of membership at GCP?

- The benefits of membership include the following. According to the GCP Constitution membership entitles "the member to vote at a meeting of the members on those matters that the Board of Elders chooses to submit to the church membership for affirmation. . ." Thus a non-member would not have the right of affirming matters presented by the Elders, such as the election and appointment of church leadership, major financial decisions, and weighty matters affecting the life of the church, such as church discipline. Matthew 18:15–17 demonstrates that involving the church body may be the final step in matters which affect church unity and purity. Without church membership there is no way to define the group that will take up these sensitive and weighty matters. This same passage provides accountability for members to a group of people which has the authority to settle disciplinary matters.

---

2. In all things we should be gracious and patient toward those with whom we disagree. We should be careful not to magnify disagreements, particularly in the area of ecclesiology and eschatology, above their Scriptural importance and/or clarity. Consider the words of J. L. Reynolds concerning his opposition to infant baptism: "On the subject of infant baptism, and what seems to me to be its legitimate tendencies, I have recorded my sentiments without reserve, and, I trust, without offence. I impeach no Man's motives; nor do I question the piety and sincerity of those of my Christian brethren who believe that the practice is sanctioned by divine command. . .. It is impossible not to admire and love men whose faith and practice associate them with Baxter, Leighton, Edwards, and Martyn, and who breathe their heavenly spirit." J.L.Reynolds, *Church Polity*.

- There are further indications of a Christian's submission to leadership in a New Testament assembly which must be preceded by some sort of expressed willingness or covenant or agreement or commitment (I Thess 5:12–13; I Tim 5:17; Heb 13:17). Membership is one way of taking these commands seriously and practically. In Acts 20:28 Paul tells the elders how to care for their flock. Of course, elders have a responsibility for unbelievers and non-members but the idea of a primacy in care for a flock should encourage Christians to be part of a defined flock for whom the elders will give an account to God.

How about those who hold to a sincere and mature belief in baptism as expressed in the Westminster Confession of Faith?

We welcome into full membership and partnership in ministry those sincere and mature believers who hold a commitment to baptism as expressed in the Westminster Confession of Faith. This does not diminish our belief in what we understand to be the Scriptural practice of believer's baptism, but rather gives fellowship in the gospel priority over other aspects of faith. In so doing we affirm that the gospel is the basis of our fellowship in Christ and service to Christ. The Elders will admit to membership those who believe that their infant baptism is both Scriptural and a matter of conscience before God, yet at the same time setting forth clearly the teaching of believer's baptism as practiced by Grace Church of Philly.

CHAPTER FORTY-FIVE

Gospel-Centered Church Leadership

ELDERS

We understand the NT to teach that the church is governed by biblically qualified men who share the responsibility of leadership. These men are affirmed by the congregation and accountable to each other. The Lead Pastor is "first-among-equals" in leadership, but "one-among-equals" in decision-making. Here are some reasons why we believe that shared leadership is both biblical and practical:[1]

- It develops and matures men in the chief virtues of brotherly love, humility, and mutual submission.
- It provides a "living model" of how the whole congregation is to live and work in mutual accord.
- It distributes burdens, conflicts, complaints, and problems of church leadership among a group of shepherding elders.
- It serves as a check and balance on each other to guard against human tendencies.

---

1. Some of these points are based on insights from Bruce Stabbert, *The Team Concept*, 69, and Timothy George, *Baptist Theologians*, 564–6.

- It allows decision-making to become a corporate leadership responsibility. No one individual calls the shots. It increases the effectiveness of the overall church ministries.
- It diminishes the conflict connected with the two-board system.
- It provides a broader and more reliable base for church leadership.
- It permits pastors/elders to be close to the people, even in larger churches.
- It allows for needed variety in the ministry.
- It provides for power in prayer amongst the leadership of the church.

DEACONS

New Testament Deacons (men and women) serve the Lord by conducting the caring ministry of the church—doing the benevolence work, visiting the sick, being alert to the spiritual needs of the congregation—and assisting the elders in other matters for the purposes of freeing the pastoral staff to focus on prayer and the ministry of the Word, promoting unity within the church, and facilitating the spread of the gospel.

SECTION EIGHT

On Social Issues

CHAPTER FORTY-SIX

Conservative or Liberal under the Lordship of Jesus Christ

I choose to live under the Lordship of Jesus Christ. This is my joyful response to His saving grace. Though I would be described as a political conservative, I hold supreme allegiance to Christ and the authority of His Word. I hold "qualified" allegiance to "conservative" values and will always evaluate those values by the Word of God. All humans are fallible; all political parties are fallible; all religious institutions are fallible; all news reporting is fallible. I denounce and disassociate from any conservative views and voices that I view as in conflict with Scripture.

Regardless of where conservatives may be, I will never agree with the legitimacy of same-sex marriage (an oxymoron) or same-sex sexual relationships or any sexual relationships outside of heterosexual marriage. I will always call them sin. I will never agree with the governmental forced redistribution of wealth. Though governments have a biblical right to a legitimate tax, they have no biblical right to confiscate honest wealth and to play Robin Hood. I will never agree with the use of lethal force and power simply for economic or personal gain, though I do accept the divine responsibility of the government to use lethal force in order to protect life. I will never agree with democracy (the majority rules), when democracy conflicts with the law of God. An evil majority is still evil. I will never agree with hateful, vile language and actions that seek to diminish the life of any human being. I will never agree with abortion.

Section Eight | On Social Issues

These are six of my basic convictions regarding public issues, two of which are inferences from biblical principles, while four are the unequivocal teaching of Scripture (as I see it). I'll leave you to figure out that breakdown.

I have Christian friends, good friends, and acquaintances who espouse a much more liberal view of government and politics. Some of them hold strong allegiance to the Democratic Party. I love them and continue to enjoy our fellowship in Christ. I think many of their political views are wrong, but they also think the same of me.

However, if we both live under the Lordship of Christ and the authority of Scripture, then we both, whether liberal or conservative, should denounce and disassociate from those views and voices within any movement that clearly are in conflict with Scripture. Living under the Lordship of Christ, we know that there is such a thing as truth and error, right and wrong, black and white, good and bad.

> [20] Woe to those who call evil good and good evil, who put darkness for light and light for darkness, who put bitter for sweet and sweet for bitter! (Isa. 5:20 ESV)

May we have the biblical insight to identify evil in both liberal and conservative movements, and may we have the courage to speak out against all that is contrary to the Lordship of Christ. Neither Donald nor Hillary is Jesus. Neither the Republican nor Democrat Party is the Kingdom of God.

Actually, we who live under the Lordship of Christ, whether liberal or conservative, should agree on many current issues in our society. We denounce evil, vile, hateful speech and acts. We denounce abortion. We denounce sex outside of heterosexual marriage. We denounce the use of power to oppress others. We denounce protesters who commit criminal acts, whose language is vile and disgraceful, whose hatred is base and violent. We denounce the diminishing of any human being, whether by lies, or defamation of character, or crude speech, or racism, or classism, or biased reporting.

More importantly, we agree on many things of ultimate importance. We agree that Jesus Christ is Savior and Lord. He alone is the Sovereign King. We agree that "there is no other name under heaven by which we must be saved." We agree that He is Truth and that His Word is Truth. We agree that the only reliable, infallible authority we have is the Bible. We believe that Christ calls us to a unique love for other believers and a powerful love that reaches out even to our enemies. We agree that the deepest problems of humanity can only be solved by the life-giving work of the Holy Spirit. We believe that the weapons of our warfare against evil are nor the weapons of this world.

Our unqualified allegiance is to King Jesus and His Word, not to a political party, not to any politician, not to the majority or minority, and not to any philosophy of life.

CHAPTER FORTY-SEVEN

The Politics of Jesus and Peter (1 Peter 2:13–25)

A Christian living in the first century faced the challenge, as we do, of how to live as a Christian in a non-Christian world. Those whom Peter addressed in Asia Minor were mindful that they were aliens of the dispersion, i.e., their loyalties belonged to the kingdom of Jesus, yet they were temporarily dwelling in this foreign world as His people.

The Roman government was not a model of justice and increasingly it became oppressive toward Christians. The institution of slavery, though having a legitimate legal purpose for the payment of debts owed to society, had also become exploitative and oppressive. Even the husband-led structure of marriages had degenerated to the abuse and oppression of women.

Christians found themselves in situations where the natural response of the heart would be to either overthrow the institutions of society which had become corrupt or escape from these institutions to a safer place.

Strikingly, Peter offers direction to believers that overturns human expectations, opening up a new way of thinking and acting. Peter does not see how resisting and overturning the structures of society can be good for the advance of the gospel. Christians are to be known for having a spirit of submission to those who are over them, even when the exercise of that authority is oppressive.

The Politics of Jesus and Peter (1 Peter 2:13–25)

Citizens, slaves, and wives who live in the midst of less-than-ideal circumstances are encouraged to stay where they are and to keep doing what is good. Peter offers the same answer to the evil that oppresses us as Jesus did: [27] *"But I say to you who hear, Love your enemies, do good to those who hate you,* [28] *bless those who curse you, pray for those who abuse you* (Luke 6). "Doing good" is more than private morality. It is a persistent public goodness in the face of evil. Christians are not to be known as rebels, revolutionaries, "anti"-everything. Peter would tell Christians in Twenty-First Century America to discard their party line politics and to do good for the benefit of all people. He would tell them to come out of their isolation where they've retreated to safety and to engage the wider society with exceptional good works. Believers are to live with a spirit of submission and a commitment to persistent good deeds that benefit the society in which they live. Their persistent goodness defies the false accusations often made against them.

Sadly, too often the energy that goes into resisting and working to overturn the abusive structures of society eviscerates the call of Jesus to love, do good, bless, and pray. Also, when Christians retreat into the safety of their cocoons, they fail to be the salt and light that enables society to see their good works and glorify their Heavenly Father. The method for advancing the kingdom of Jesus is contrary to the world's method. Instead of resisting or escaping, Christians are called to incarnate gospel values in the midst of the evil they face.

To live in such a way calls us to a deeper faith and reflection on the cross. This is where Peter takes us. Our hearts resist living God's way because we find it difficult to believe that submission and persistent goodness can accomplish anything. Peter says, "Look at the passion of Jesus Christ." Jesus is the example of non-resistance, submission, doing good, blessing, praying, loving, and obeying even to the death of the cross. And, what did it accomplish? The redemption of the world. The model of the cross is the pattern for how we engage the structures of society that often become oppressive.

> Rejected, not a complaint
> Suffering, thirsty and faint

Section Eight | On Social Issues

Obedient, graceful restraint
He is my Savior.
Innocent, knowing no crime
Forsaken, a dreadful time
Risen, victory sublime
He is my Savior

CHAPTER FORTY-EIGHT

Seven reasons why I do not join the popular, secular fight against racism!

Yes, I write this as a white man, who has been a racist in the past, who seeks to experience gospel grace to fight internal racism in the present, and who believes that the gospel alone can resolve the evil of the human heart which fosters racism. Here are seven reasons why I do not join the popular, secular, fight against racism.

1. I do not believe we can have redeemed structures and institutions within society without having redeemed individuals. The conversion of Nicodemus, the religious leader, and Matthew, the tax collector, are good examples for me of how Jesus engaged the evil religious and political structures of his day
2. The depersonalization of evil by focusing on systemic evil undercuts and confuses the purpose of the gospel which is to redeem sinners and bring them together in one body. Systemic evil exists only because there are individuals who embody and institutionalize that evil. Whether that embodiment of evil is depravity or demonic influence, it is still individuals who foster that evil. Temporal societies and institutions are not redeemed; individuals are.
3. We do not wrestle with and defeat individuals, institutions, principalities and powers through political and societal means. The weapons of our warfare are not fleshly uses of

Section Eight | On Social Issues

power through protest, riot, or legislation, but the gospel declaration, commitment, and assurance that Jesus Christ has triumphed over the powers of evil

4. The energy and resources given to battle the symptoms of evil, such as racism, dilute the mission of the church to make disciples of all nations. I do not believe there is a better answer for racism than making disciples and nurturing churches that unite a diversity of peoples in Christ.
5. I do not desire to promote and participate in a narrative amplified by those who reject the Lordship of Christ and do not reflect the grace of God. My narrative seeks to be gospel-centered, grace-oriented, God-focused.
6. I am committed to the church of Jesus Christ, which alone is a counter-kingdom with structures that should reflect the grace of God. I have the joy of being a part of Grace Church of Philly where the gospel is bringing together whites, African-Americans, Latinos, East and West Africans and more.
7. I cannot join with others in a battle when we do not see a common enemy, do not have a common commander, and have a different war manual.

CHAPTER FORTY-NINE

Sandy Hook and the Gospel

When we look at the Sandy Hook tragedy, the question we should be asking is "what is wrong with humanity that we can commit such atrocities"? If the discussion does not go beyond "gun control" or "mental health" then our solutions will be superficial. People murder other people because they choose to unleash their hate, their anger, and their envy.

The Ten Commandments clearly condemn murder and most of us are content to live within the Sixth Commandment. However, in the Sermon on the Mount Jesus unpacks that commandment for us and shows us that murder begins in the heart with anger and hatred. Society and civil authority do their best to restrain murder; they are powerless to restrain anger, hatred, and envy. We are personally powerless to overcome anger, hate, and envy.

The truth is that all of us have experienced and tolerated a bit of anger, hate, and envy in our own hearts. We live with racism, class warfare, religious hatred, national and ethnic pride, offending and being offended, etc. Though we are restrained from murder by social pressure, self-discipline, fear of consequences, and lack of opportunity, the seeds of murder have been sown in all of our hearts.

Jesus Christ did not come simply to ensure a "murder-free" society. He came to change hearts and transform lives. He came to show us and teach us how to love God and love others, even to love our enemies. But, He came for more than that. He came to defeat Satan who is a "murderer from the beginning" and whose murderous path we are inclined to follow. He came to break the power that sin has over our hearts causing us to think more of ourselves rather than God and others. He came to conquer death so that we can live without the fear of losing this world and the stuff of this world, knowing that we have the world to come. His death and resurrection assure us that He is victorious in what He came to accomplish.

It was anger, hate, and envy that filled the crowd as they forced Jesus to the cross, crying "Crucify Him." Yes, Jesus, the Innocent One was murdered with such intense hatred and anger that no gun control legislation or mental health system could have rescued him from the intensity of human evil.

Adam Lanza's horrendous evil act reminds us of what is wrong with humanity. Evil exists in all of us. At times it may be restrained and confined to the inner life; at times it might lash out in in more acceptable forms; at times it reveals itself in unfettered horror. Evil exists.

The grace of God at work in our lives diminishes anger, hate, and envy. The work of the Holy Spirit creates an experience of God's love that enables us to love in ways we never thought possible.

If Adam Lanza had known and experienced the grace of God and the transforming power of the Holy Spirit, we would be discussing a better story. This is why we continue to preach the gospel.

CHAPTER FIFTY

"as a matter of fairness"

> [13] For I do not mean that others should be eased and you burdened, but that as a matter of fairness [14] your abundance at the present time should supply their need, so that their abundance may supply your need, that there may be fairness. [15] As it is written, "Whoever gathered much had nothing left over, and whoever gathered little had no lack" (2 Cor 9).

Is there a biblical call and example for Christians and churches with greater resources to share those resources with people and churches that have need? Has the personal pursuit of the "good life" and the obsession with "bigger and better" in American Christianity not only deterred Christians and churches from their obligation to the poor in general but also caused them to disregard the needs of people and churches in impoverished areas? The answer to both questions is resoundingly, YES!

When you are located on the border of a one of the poorest cities in the country, is raising money to remake your youth room really a legitimate home mission project? When you have a choice with your youth group to spend big bucks on a wilderness adventure or help in an urban mission project, which do you choose? When church growth demands more space, do you think about more bucks and buildings or alternatives that meet the need but share resources with poorer churches?

Perhaps some will say that my musings are driven by envy. I am not immune to that. I have in the past lived and ministered in insulation and isolation from the needy people and churches of this world. I have bought suburban property and built buildings without any regard to the needs of urban churches. Don't get me wrong. I am not adverse to creature comforts. I enjoy as many of them as I can whenever I can. But, the gospel provokes an inner tension between what I have and what others need. I have not resolved the tension but I do seek theological and practical resolutions to work out this good gospel tension.

Believers and churches in poorer areas are not looking for charity. They are looking for community with and love from others within the church of Jesus Christ. What distinguishes the world's charitable acts from the church's charitable acts is that the church seeks community with those to whom it gives. Whether it is giving to the poor outside the church or giving to believers and churches, the gospel goal is always community. In our giving to the unchurched poor we seek their inclusion in the family of God and their fellowship at the Lord's Table. In our giving to poorer believers and churches we seek to demonstrate and advance the loving community which the church of Jesus Christ should model to a watching world.

When more affluent believers and churches disregard the needs of those with less, their self-interest undercuts the promise of the gospel. Our culture tells us that success is measured by how much more we have acquired for ourselves in life; the gospel tells us that success is measured in how much we have given away.

When we have seen and felt the emptiness of building personal and church empires and worldly monuments of success, then our use of what we have will always be in consideration of "do not forget the poor."

When that happens, affluent Christians will not simply practice "arm's length" charity but will seek the kind of loving community in which "fairness" is a biblical ideal.

As the gospel strips away our secular values of success, the day will come when more affluent suburban churches are tied to intimate community with urban churches and Third World churches in which "fairness" is a growing reflection of the gospel at work.

Bibliography

Achtemeier, Paul J. *First Peter* in *Hermeneia*. Minneapolis: Fortress, 1996.
Baxter, Richard. Quoted by Elyse Fitzpatrick and Dennis Johnson in *Counsel from the Cross*. Wheaton: Crossway Books, 2009.
Callahan, Kennon. *Effective Church Leadership*. Hoboken, NJ: Josey-Bass, 1990.
Compton, Andrew. *Reformed Reader*. http://tinyurl.com/7rh6n6s.
"Constitution of Grace Church of Philly." https://www.gracechurchphilly.org/wp-content/uploads/2019/12/Constitution-2020.pdf.
Edgar, William. *Worship in All of Life*. https://students.wts.edu/resources/westminsterspeaks/2003/01/01/Worship_In_All_of_Life.html.
Evangelicals & Catholics Together. https://www.firstthings.com/article/1994/05/evangelicals-catholics-together-the-christian-mission-in-the-third-millennium.
George, Timothy and Dockery, David, eds. *Baptist Theologians*. Nashville: Baptist Sunday School Board, 1990.
Goldsworthy, Graeme. According to Plan. Leicester: IVP, 1991.
Hodge, A. A. *Outlines of Theology*. Carlisle, PA: Banner of Truth, 1972.
Jenson, Robert W. "How the World Lost Its Story." *First Things* (Oct. 93) 19.
Johnson, Philip E. "Nihilism and the End of Law." *First Things* (March 1993) 19.
Lindsell, Harold. *The Battle for the Bible*. Grand Rapids: Zondervan, 1976.
MacArthur, John. "The Glory of the New Covenant." https://www.gty.org/library/sermons-library/47-21/the-glory-of-the-new-covenant-part-7.
McCune, Roland. "The New Evangelicalism: Evaluation and Prospects." *DBSJ* 8 (Fall 2003) 85–99.
Mohler, Albert. *Election*. http://www.albertmohler.com/documents/Mohler_opening_comments_for_election_discussion_2006_Pastors_Conference.pdf.
Packer, J. I. *Rediscovering Holiness*. Delight, AR: Gospel Light, 1973.
Piper, John. *Desiring God*. Colorado Springs: Multnomah Books,
Poythress, Vern. *The Shadow of Christ in the Law of Moses*. Phillipsburg, NJ: P&R, 1995.
Reynolds, J. L. "Church Polity or the Kingdom of Christ." https://founders.org/polity/church-polity-or-the-kingdom-of-christ-reynolds/.

Bibliography

Sisk, John. *First Things* (May 1993) 9.
Slick, Mark. "What are Pelagianism and Semi-Pelagianism." http://www.carm.org/heresy/pelagianism.htm.
Stabbert. Bruce. *The Team Concept*. Hegg Brothers, 1982.
Towards Common Witness. https://www.oikoumene.org/resources/documents/towards-common-witness.
Van Til, Cornelius. *An Introduction to Systematic Theology*. Phillipsburg, NJ: P&R Publishing, 1974.

www.ingramcontent.com/pod-product-compliance
Lightning Source LLC
Chambersburg PA
CBHW051058160426
43193CB00010B/1232